LOVE IN SPAIN,

AND

OTHER POEMS.

BY

MARTHA PERRY LOWE,

AUTHOR OF "THE OLIVE AND THE PINE."

BOSTON:

WILLIAM V. SPENCER,

203, WASHINGTON STREET.

1867.

CAMBRIDGE:
PRESS OF JOHN WILSON AND SON.

CONTENTS.

LOVE IN SPAIN.

MISCELLANEOUS POEMS.

THE SHADOW OVER THE LAND.

LOVE IN SPAIN.

DRAMATIS PERSONÆ.

MANUEL, *Duke of Alancia.*

SIR HENRY IVERTON, *English Minister to Spain.*

EVERARD, *Secretary of Legation.*

DON FERMIN MORALES, *friend to Alancia.*

ELEANOR MANTON, *niece to Sir Henry.*

LADY IVERTON, *wife of Sir Henry.*

DOÑA MARIA, DE ALANCIA, *mother to the Duke.*

CHRISTINA, *Queen-mother.*

ANITA, *Countess of Lozano.*

JUANA, *maid to Eleanor.*

PART I.

SCENE I.—MADRID.

In the Puerta del Sol. A knot of common Spaniards talking in the street.

FIRST SPANIARD.

Ah, buenas dias! Parco, how fare you?

SECOND SPANIARD.

Oh, well enough, as goes the jogging world!
I came through yonder street, and caught a breeze
That froze me stiff as ice. I turned in here
To thaw myself again.

THIRD SPANIARD.

Upon my word,
Hermano, you are yellow as a lemon.

FOURTH SPANIARD.

He will not feel much sun this morning. Whew!
I'd like to run down south a dozen leagues.

[*Shrugs his shoulders.*

THIRD SPANIARD.

Carámba! I should like to see you stir
Enough for that; you never got beyond
The Prado, in your very longest walks.

FIRST SPANIARD.

Well, well, amigos; let us be content;
The winter's flying merrily away.
Who wants to run about and tire his bones?

SECOND SPANIARD.

Ay, ay, my son; you are content, indeed.
Your moza's eyes are warming you enough.
Ah, ha; she gave me such a pretty look,
One day, when old Josepha's back was turned!

FIRST SPANIARD (*hotly*).

How now, my man? What mean you, picaro?

SECOND SPANIARD.

Soft, soft, amigo! I was joking only,
To get your blood in easy circulation.

[*He sees a girl with chestnuts.*

Hola, there's Mariquita with her nuts!

[*He beckons to her.*

S'st! Mariquita, let us see thy eyes.

GIRL (*comes along coquettishly, with her head aside*).

Gracias, señores, if you take the nuts.

SECOND SPANIARD.

Ea, ea! my Niña; one look first.

[*They examine the nuts, and take up handsfull.*

FOURTH SPANIARD.

How much?

GIRL.

Ah! one peséta; that is all.

FOURTH SPANIARD.

Too much,
Too much, I tell you. Here's enough.

[*Handing her money.*

GIRL.

No, no!
You cheat me now, señores.

THIRD SPANIARD.

Come, come, come!
Adios, Mariquita, so bonita.

[*Throwing her money. She smiles, and moves along. She meets an old woman with oranges.*

OLD WOMAN.

Por Dios, child! You will not earn your garlic
While you are chaffering with those pollos there.
They're making sport, my girl. I warrant ye,
I keep me clear of them.

GIRL.

Bueno, madre;
You're not so young as you were once, I guess.

OLD WOMAN (*going on her way*).

The saucy puss! But I remember how
I used to put geraniums in my hair,
And step as neat as she. Ay, well-a-day.
My hair is grisly now; but by and by
It will be white, and then the scarlet flowers
Will show as well as in that little jade's.

[*She goes on, crying her oranges.*

Na - - - ran - - - ja - - - das - - -
Muy - - - fres - - - cas.

SECOND SPANIARD.

Amigos, see the ladies coming out!

THIRD SPANIARD.

There is a troop of brisk Inglesas yonder.
I know their stride a half a league from here.

FOURTH SPANIARD.

See their mantillas, square upon their backs!
They move along like red-faced jointed dolls,
Who dare not turn their heads to right nor left.

THIRD SPANIARD.

There's one behind the rest who's graciosa;
I think she comes from the Ambassador's.

FIRST SPANIARD.

Yes, she is passable.

[*A Spanish woman approaches.*

THIRD SPANIARD.

Hola! hola!
A pretty girl!

[*She passes. They all look.*

(*Aloud.*)

What beauty! Senorita,
You are too preciosa for these streets;
You'll wet your little feet.

FOURTH SPANIARD.

I'll take my oath
She is no Madridlena.

THIRD SPANIARD.

That's she not!
I'll wager she's from Cadiz; know ye, hombres?

[*He starts after her, singing.*

"Ay, for me the Gaditana,
She's of all the world sultana."

[*A beggar runs up, holding out his hand.*

BEGGAR.

Give, señor, and the Virgin, — she will pay you.

THIRD SPANIARD.

Por Dios, brother, pardon me, I pray!

[*Beggar retires.*

The Virgin will not stop *her;* there she goes.
The rascal thrust his swarthy face between,
Just as she tripped it jaunty round the corner.

[*He follows round, and disappears. The other Spaniards retire. Two gentlemen appear.*

DON FERMIN MORALES.

How is it, Jose, with the Liberals?
They say there is a league on foot; is't true?
Tut, tut; you redden at the question. So?
You hold the stirrups of the party, eh?

DON JOSE DE LEON.

Thank you, señor; I'm no man's lackey yet.

DON FERMIN.

Well, well! 'twill end in smoke, save that a few
Good heads will fall. I pray you, keep your own.

DON JOSE.

And which is best, — to keep your precious head
And let a nation grovel in the dust;
Or lose your head, that men may walk upright?

DON FERMIN.

You'll lose your head, and leave them in the mire.
Some of the bluest blood of Spain, they say,
Is compromised. I've heard Alancia's name, —
The duke, — they will not draw him in, I think;

He's seen the thing in Italy and France.
Moreover, he has far too much to lose.

DON JOSE.

We are no better off than with Narvaez.
He ruled us with a rod of iron, truly;
But we knew where we were when he was leader.

DON FERMIN.

What can you make out of Murillo's speeches?

DON JOSE.

I make out one thing, that he means to tax us.

DON FERMIN.

He's so long-winded, he forgets the errand
He started on, before he ends his speech.

DON JOSE.

He don't forget one thing, you may be certain:
He means to keep up the old despotism.

DON FERMIN.

He is hard-pressed between the Moderados —
You must confess it — and you Progresistas.

DON JOSE.

We'd like to squeeze him just a little harder,
And rid the country of him altogether.

SCENE II.

Ball in the palace of the Queen-mother, CHRISTINA. SIR HENRY IVERTON; EVERARD; ELEANOR; LADIES *and* GENTLEMEN.

EVERARD.

I hope I see you well to-night, Sir Henry.
There are no further news from England yet?

SIR HENRY.

No, not a single word. Slow way it has,
To travel over these old Pyrenees,
That shut us from the habitable world;
I'm wearied out, Heaven knows it, moping here,
Away from all they're doing in the North. —
You mark I've some old British stuff still left.

EVERARD.

That would be hard for you to lose, Sir Henry.

SIR HENRY.

I pray you, no example take by me.
You see I have not learned, in these two years,
A diplomat's first part, — to hold his tongue.

EVERARD.

One of your most renownēd predecessors
Would not have got his tongue so badly burned,

If he had meddled with the broth so little.
I do not fear to follow you, Sir Henry,
Who keep yourself so firm on every side.

SIR HENRY.

What do you think about this Liberal movement?

EVERARD.

I think it moonshine; nothing else, Sir Henry.
'Twill never reach the height of revolution;
Or, if it does, 'twill burst up at the crisis.

SIR HENRY.

And yet they have some honest men among them.

EVERARD.

It may be, but they have no force at bottom.
'Tis the same game they're always playing here.
The government is up, and they are down;
Then they are up, and falls the Cabinet.
Just so it was through all the Carlist days, —
Christina and the powers at hide-and-seek.
Until they fairly drove out Espartero,
And old Narvaez managed things himself.

SIR HENRY.

Well, well; 'tis good to have the waters moving:
'Tis better for the world than dull stagnation.

EVERARD.

They keep them pretty muddy, that is certain.

SIR HENRY.

We have to tread about us softly here;
We know not what we're coming down upon.
But you are just the man to steer with me
Through these thick waters; just the man for Spain.

EVERARD.

Sir Henry, I am sure you do me honor,
In placing so much confidence in me.

SIR HENRY.

No, not a bit; but there are some, you know,
Who're always stepping on their neighbor's toes,
And thereby putting out of joint their own.
I wish I could sit down and have a chat
On old familiar scenes; but Eleanor, —

[ELEANOR *approaches.*

Ah! here she is, — my niece; you've met before;
She will point out the notorieties.

[SIR HENRY *retires.*

EVERARD (*turning towards her and bowing*).

I think I had the pleasure once to meet you
Among the silver lakes of Cumberland?

ELEANOR.

Yes, I remember; quite another scene
We witness in these foreign rooms to-night.

EVERARD.

Yes, art and nature; but you will confess
The former always charms the ladies best.
These coronets, these diamonds, — do not they
Outshine the little mountain lakes at home?

ELEANOR.

That is a weighty question. Pardon me,
I have no time nor skill to answer it,
Amid this thronging company to-night;
Besides, how mad to talk of diamonds
When all these Spanish eyes are flashing round:
Where is your English gallantry, I pray?

EVERARD.

How ladies will evade an open question!

ELEANOR.

We will not throw our sentiment away,
When doubt is creeping o'er the questioner's face.
Look yonder! that gay lady talking there
Is Alva's handsome duchess; mark her well, —
She reigns supreme in beauty, rank, and fashion.
That is the Duke of Riensares there,
Against the wall: do you not think he has
A very noble head, a lordly air?

EVERARD.

Though not of lords. Yes, true, indeed he has.
The Queen Christina certainly is kind
To let him talk with all the ladies here.

ELEANOR.

He is the only one she would not rule.

EVERARD.

Because she could not, I suppose.

ELEANOR.

No, no.
They say she really married him for love;
Is proud of having such a handsome husband.
You look incredulous; but do not try
To challenge me again to argument.

EVERARD (*smiling*).

Then, will you walk into the other room?
[*He gives her his arm, and they disappear.*

SCENE III.

The same. Another room of the palace. ANITA, *Countess of Lozano.* SPANISH LADIES. GENTLEMAN.

FIRST LADY.

Dost know Don Manuel is come back again
From all his journeys into foreign lands?

Hear'st thou the news, Anita? Dost thou hear?
He called thee pretty; thou rememberest that?

ANITA.

What say'st thou? Who?

FIRST LADY.

Who? why, Alancia.

ANITA.

Ah! yes, I know; but he's not here to-night.

SECOND LADY.

He's been in France; he'll not come early now.

ANITA.

Nor dance.

FIRST LADY.

No, he'll like nothing now in Spain.
They say that he has grown so handsome, too,
That all the ladies here are dying for him.
And he is turned a poet; he writes books!

ANITA.

Ah, Concha, how he used to dance with me!

FIRST LADY.

'Tis grown the fashion to be dull as sheep.
Cáspita! did you see them stand around,

When we were at the French Ambassador's,
And stare each other in the face like owls?

ANITA.

Oh, but the Paris dresses were so sweet!

LADY.

Yes, yes; and that was all there was of them.
A row of dresses spread upon the sofa,
Until some gibbering pair of pantaloons
Came up and bowed, and talked in broken Spanish,
Or foreign jargon never made for Christians.
O Dios, save me from these elegantes!
And save me from a diplomatic party.
But yet these madames, with their languid airs,
Keep all the married and the single men.
   Bless me! I'm glad I married my Francisco;
I never should have got him if I'd waited.

ANITA.

Ah, how Valencia used to dance with me!
I care not what he does, if he will dance.
He said I had the lightest foot in town.

FIRST LADY.

Dance, girl! art mad? What cares he for thy foot?
He writes, he writes.

ANITA.

                              And so does Pedro, too.
He writes me verses; he's no worse for it.

FIRST LADY.

Pedro, indeed!

ANITA (*beckoning*).

Pedro, come hither; quick

[*He approaches.*

PEDRO.

Fairest condésa, I am at your feet.

ANITA.

I kiss my hands to you, my good Don Pedro.
Is't true Don Manuel mopes with pen and ink?

FIRST LADY.

Say, Pedro, is it true that our Infanta,
The Duchess of Montpensier, in Sevilla,
Has asked Alancia to her boudoir,
And heard him read his dramas?

GENTLEMAN.

Ay, and more;
Montpensier sends the book to all his friends;
You know he likes to tickle Spanish pride.

ANITA (*starting*).

Pedro, Pedro! dost hear the music sounding?

GENTLEMAN.

Mazurka? Ay, ay, little one; I come.

[*They go into the dancing hall.*

SCENE IV.

The same. Another room of the palace. Queen Christina. Don Manuel de Alancia. *The Duke enters the room, and approaches the Queen, bowing low.*

QUEEN CHRISTINA.

You have been absent many months from Spain.

ALANCIA.

A year, your majesty.

QUEEN.

Welcome to you.

ALANCIA (*bowing*).

Your majesty does me the greatest honor.

QUEEN.

How fares it with you, duke, since your return?
Have any foreign countries won your heart,
Or are you still of us in our good Spain?

ALANCIA.

I never can be other than a Spaniard, —
Your majesty knows that.

QUEEN.

And you have been
In our fair Naples, too. How looked it; gay?

ALANCIA.

Most gay, your majesty. And there I thought
How favored Spain, so many years, has worn
Upon her head their royal native gem.

QUEEN.

Our thanks, Valencia; you've learned to use
The courtliness of Neapolitans.

ALANCIA.

A Spaniard need not learn to speak the truth,
Need he, señora?

QUEEN.

Ah, the poet's eye
Did prompt the thought, perchance.

ALANCIA.

That suits me more
Please you, señora; for the poet speaks
What he believes: his teacher is his heart.

QUEEN.

When may we have the pleasure, señor duke,
To taste the inspiration from your pen?

ALANCIA (*bowing low*).

Whene'er your majesty will honor me.

QUEEN.

We love the Spanish verse: it has a touch
Of fire unknown to soft Italian bards;
It harps not sickly over hapless lovers,
But speaks of glory, danger, and of death.

ALANCIA (*with low, earnest voice*).

Señora, I am full of graver thoughts. —

[*More noble guests approach. He is forced to retire, bowing low.*

SCENE V.

The same. In another apartment of the palace. ALANCIA, *and his friend* DON FERMIN MORALES.

DON FERMIN (*whispering*).

What, in the name of Heaven, will you do?

ALANCIA.

Do? we will overturn this Ministry.
Will you go with us? Answer yea, or nay.

DON FERMIN.

I'll go, and keep your head upon your neck.

ALANCIA.

I'd rather take my chance, by half, without you.

DON FERMIN.

Come, come; you must bestir you, Manuel!
Yon little countess there is all a flutter;
The mother has been looking sharp for you,
This many a day. Go up, and do your duty.

ALANCIA.

The little Anita! Saint Isidro!
And is that she? How pretty she is grown!

[DON FERMIN *pulls him along.*

(ALANCIA *whispers.*)

Stay, stay a moment! Who is that?

DON FERMIN.

The tall one?

ALANCIA.

No, no; she leans upon the window-seat.

DON FERMIN.

She? Oh, that is the Señorita Manton.
Her uncle is the British Minister.
She has of late come out to him in Spain.
They call her handsome; but she has no dowry.

ALANCIA.

No dowry! Heavens, with such a neck, such eyes.
No dowry! Ha! wait, Fermin, but a moment.
Can you not introduce me to the lady?

[*Pulling away.*

There is Sir Henry; I'll pay my respects.

[*He goes towards him.*

DON FERMIN.

Ha, ha! I'll bet his liberal game is quashed.

[*He goes off laughing.* SIR HENRY *and* ALANCIA *leave the room together.*

SCENE VI.

The same. SIR HENRY *and* ALANCIA *return together.* SIR HENRY *presents the Duke to his niece, and retires.*

ALANCIA (*bowing*).

Fair señorita, I am at your feet.
It shames me not to speak your native tongue.

ELEANOR.

Wherefore, I pray, señor?

ALANCIA.

All men should know it.
I fear to prove we Spaniards are as slow
At learning foreign speech, as foreign fashion;
Moreover, I would have the lady choose
The language we should speak together in, —
Her own, or mine.

ELEANOR.

I choose the Spanish, then,
Because it is most beautiful, señor;
And also, I would learn to speak it well.
[*Interrupting him as he begins to speak.*
Señor, say not, like all the Spanish men,
I speak it to perfection.

ALANCIA.

Señorita,
I will not be like all the rest. I'll say
I would *not* have you speak it perfectly;
It would not sound one half so charmingly.
Believe me, señorita, I do love
The Spanish from a foreign lady's tongue;
We clip it now of half its stately grace.
'Tis like an olden garment thrown around
A finer form; 'tis new and fresh again,
And hangs in folds of grace we give it not.
[*He starts, looking at an open window behind them.*
Is not the night air cold for you?

ELEANOR.

O no.

ALANCIA.

'Tis true, indeed, they say the northern winds
But warm the roses on the British cheek;
And yet our breezes from the Guadarramas
Are not like those across the misty sea.

ELEANOR.

Your sun can give a richer glow, señor,
Than all the freshness of the wintry North;
But yet the ladies in Madrid are pale.

ALANCIA.

Yes, Madrid is a chilly place at best.
You have not been in Andalusia yet?

ELEANOR.

Not yet. I dream of it by night and day.

ALANCIA.

I've journeyed many leagues from home of late,
But, when I saw again my native shore,
My soul was warm and glowing as a boy.

ELEANOR.

What did you, when you first came back to Spain?

ALANCIA.

I looked all day upon the azure sea
Of Malaga, and up the hoary rocks
Where our sad Moors once sat in gay content,
Until they felt the touch of Spanish sword.
I lingered in the white Alhambra courts,
Until the tumult of the busy world
Did fade away amid my pleasant dreams,

I waking but to hear beneath my feet
The Darro gurgling softly with the notes
Of nightingales that answered all around,
Within the lonely thicket shading soft
The fair Sultana's royal chamber there.
And then I sailed along the smiling banks
Of Guadalquivir, famed in love and war,—
Where are the far-renownēd orange groves,
All gleaming out in cooling green and gold,
Coquetting with the thirsty voyageur.
At last I reached Sevilla's charmēd gates,—
You, señorita, know perchance what we
Do dare to call our beautiful Sevilla?

ELEANOR.

The "Wonder of the world."

ALANCIA.

True; sounds it vain?
Poor Spain must ever boast of what she *has*,
No longer now of what she *is* and *does*;
I've been in many a gay metropolis,
But none has such a power as sweet Sevilla.
I beg your pardon for this rambling talk.

ELEANOR.

No, no; go on, señor.

ALANCIA.

'Tis not alone
Her palace, nor her flowery promenades;
Nor the Padilla's roofs of arabesque,
With bright mosaic, rainbow-tinted walls;
Nor the gay courts that gleam along the streets;
The old Giralda, mellow in the sun;
Nor yet the great cathedral. No; 'tis all.

ELEANOR.

You'll make me very discontent, señor;
Your pictures waken longings in my heart
I cannot satisfy for many a day.
The word Sevilla long has been a charm
To fire the romance of the northern blood.

ALANCIA.

The Spanish ladies care not for such things.
How I would like to show these spots to you!

ELEANOR.

Thanks. You've not been in England, I believe?

ALANCIA.

Yes, señorita, I have travelled there.
How lovely and how fresh the country is;
Ah! we have no such trees in Spain as those.

ELEANOR.

It is a glorious country, true, señor;
I shall forget Sevilla, if you praise
My home as well. What will you say of London?

ALANCIA.

I was amazed with all its strength and greatness;
But then I was a helpless foreigner.
I felt me like a child; I could not ask
Ev'n for my bread and cup of chocolate.

ELEANOR.

The chocolate, I fear me, looked so thin,
Your blood ran chill, and you were sick for Spain.

ALANCIA.

Your pardon, fair Inglesa; I confess
The truthfulness of what you say to me.
A Spaniard may admire, — and God forbid
That he should be so narrow built of soul,
As not to feel the glories of your land;
But he has his peculiar way of speech:
He thinks and acts after an olden fashion;
He walks and sits as centuries have taught.
Take him away, and he is nothing then, —
A miserable, grovelling foreigner.

ELEANOR (*smiling*).

I am most glad, señor, you haply left
The blighting mildew of our northern shores,
Before it fell on you.

ALANCIA.

Fair señorita,
I pray you pardon my ungallant speech;
It is no fault of England, but ourselves.
We Spaniards are a most unpliant race,—
Too redolent of all the past, to live
Beneath the daylight of your wondrous present.
But tell me how you live there, señorita?
What is your home like? what do you love most?

ELEANOR.

I? Oh, I love the woods, the deep green woods;
The old grey towers, with ivy all o'ergrown;
The long, long walks on pleasant July mornings,
Sitting upon the hillside with my book,
Or, better far, my friend to talk with me.

ALANCIA.

Your friend? I hope he comprehended well
His happiness. Is he not lonely now?
How I do pity him.

ELEANOR.

Ah! spare yourself;
'Twas my sweet sister cousin, whom I named.

ALANCIA.

Your cousin? Looks she then like you?

ELEANOR.

She? no.
Her eyes are black as night. If she were here,
You'd say she was a lovely Spanish lady.

ALANCIA.

Ah! then 'tis surely better that kind fate
Has sent you, señorita, in her stead,
To give us now a glimmering of the light
Like what we see around the golden heads
Of pictured saints, but never in our world.

ELEANOR.

You have not seen her, so you cannot tell.

ALANCIA.

I've seen the light, and I am satisfied.
But are you not afraid to wander there,
Within the forests, with your black-eyed friend?
What if you met some handsome cavalier?

ELEANOR.

He'd touch his hat, and pass us by, señor.

ALANCIA.

What if there were some brigand by the way?

ELEANOR.

We have no gentlemen so rare, señor.

ALANCIA.

Ah! I begin to like your England now.
The cavalier of whom we lately spoke,
Can he not say a word as he is passing?

ELEANOR.

Maybe he will, if he look young and gay,
Is not a creeping, dried-up botanist,
Or sportsman, thinking only of his dogs.

ALANCIA.

And are you not affrighted at his words?

ELEANOR.

Not if he seem a courteous gentleman.

ALANCIA.

And he will show you where the flowers grow,
And bring you water from the brook, perhaps.
Ah! surely I have not seen England yet —
If I had wandered in the British woods,
Should I have met fair ladies hand in hand,
With gold and raven curls together mingling?

[*A servant passes by with ices.*

Will you not have refreshments, señorita,
After the charming ramble 'mong the hills?

ELEANOR.

I thank you: no; I see my aunt approach
To say the hour of leaving comes. Good-night.

[*He bows, and they all retire.*

SCENE VII.

ELEANOR *and* LADY IVERTON *in their carriage.*

LADY IVERTON (*yawning*).

The ball was rather dull to-night, I think;
What say you of it?

ELEANOR.

'Twas not dull to me;
It was a charming night. But then, you know,
I am a novice here.

LADY IVERTON.

Who was the Spaniard
That you were talking with when I came up?
I have forgotten.

ELEANOR.

Do you not remember?
The duke, — Don Manuel de Alancia.

LADY IVERTON.

Yes, yes; he is a handsome man, I think.

[*She falls asleep.*

ELEANOR (*to herself*).

Yes, he *is* handsome, that none could deny.
I should have known he was a poet, too;
He compliments like all the southern men —
And yet he's different; I'll not believe
He says the same to every woman here.
O, silly girl! your head is turned already.
I wonder if he stays at home this winter;
They say he's going to marry Anita,
The little countess. How absurd, how foolish!
What is she? She is pretty; yes, no more.
She has high rank, and money too, they say.
I wonder how I looked: when I was dressed,
Aunt Margaret praised me more than is her wont,
And good Juana clapped her hands in glee.
What glowing pictures were they which he drew!
He was not talking merely to be heard;
I think he had no other way to speak.
How delicate, respectful, chivalrous!
He calls to mind those knights in old romance.
I wish I knew an Englishman like him.

[*The sound of the porter unbarring the heavy iron door, arouses her from her reverie. They alight, and go in.*

PART II.

SCENE I.

An alley of Madrid. Three SPANIARDS *wrapped in their cloaks. Night.*

FIRST SPANIARD.

Do you, Manuel de Alancia, swear to go hand in hand with us?

ALANCIA.

I swear!

FIRST SPANIARD.

You are young.

ALANCIA.

I shall be older.

FIRST SPANIARD.

You are a poet.

ALANCIA.

I am a man.

FIRST SPANIARD.

You are noble.

ALANCIA.

The people shall be noble.

FIRST SPANIARD.

Your life is sweet to lose.

ALANCIA.

Not sweeter than honorable death to gain.

SECOND SPANIARD.

Things look rather dark before us yet.

ALANCIA.

Whom have you to count upon in the opposition?

SECOND SPANIARD.

Escosura we may rely on. Narvaez was rather unguarded when he let him come back from banishment.

ALANCIA.

He did no more harm while the duke was in power. I have seen him applaud Escosura myself when he was speaking.

SECOND SPANIARD.

Yes; but things are changed now. He is a brilliant antagonist.

ALANCIA.

What do you think of Valdegamas?

SPANIARD.

He is too high-flown to have much practical influence one way or the other.

ALANCIA (*smiling*).

His marquis title, I suppose you think, has spoiled him.

SPANIARD.

Well, I don't know; a Moderado doesn't change his colors any quicker at a marquisate, than a Progresista at a countship.

ALANCIA.

Human nature is about the same in all ranks.

SPANIARD.

Justamente!

[*Exeunt.*

SCENE II.

After some days. ELEANOR *alone at home, looking at a basket of flowers.*

ELEANOR.

How beautiful these blushing roses are!
And this white jessamine; I love it best.

[*She smells of it.*

That little bit, that used to climb so high
Upon our Northern wall, would stare at these.
How we protected it from all the cold,
And watched it budding out afresh in spring!

Oh! I remember now; I said one night
How much I loved it, though 'twas not to *him.*
He heard, and brought a sprig to *me.* 'Tis he,
I know, I know. Aunt thinks 'tis Everard.
Everard! how foolish! I should like to see
A sprig of jessamine within his hand;
Would he dare give a flower to a lady?
He might involve himself in gallantries,
And lose his air of high indifference.
He seems to come here willingly enough;
Uncle does urge him so.

[*She looks at the flowers.*

Alancia —
How handsome he was looking yesterday,
As he rode by us on the Prado walks!

[*She discovers a slip of paper, and reads.*

Lady, thou art very fair;
Gold with blue of heaven vies,
Floating in thy lustrous hair,
Deep'ning in thy starry eyes.

Art thou spirit of the light,
Sent from Paradise to men, —
To the dusky sons of night?
Ah! be kind as angels then.

Take these flowers: in them lie
Sweet hopes, blended with a sigh.
They are full of visions sweet;
Will they speed me to thy feet?

Tell me, lady, were it well,
Left I them my tale to tell?
Better were their charm unbroken,
Better were my love unspoken?

[*She starts.*

Hark! who is that? It must be Everard.

[*She hides the paper. He enters, salutes her, and seats himself.*

EVERARD.

So you've been walking out to-day, I see,
By all these flowers.

ELEANOR.

No; I have not been out.

EVERARD.

Some wretched youth, whom you've ensnared, has sent them.

ELEANOR.

Just as you please; I do not know myself.

EVERARD.

Ah! mystery it is, Miss Eleanor, —
A source of greatest pleasure to your sex.
They're well arranged; but I cannot profess
To any knowledge of the bouquet art.

ELEANOR.

Yes: they are very tastefully combined.

4

EVERARD.

How all these men do revel here in show,
Be it the meeting of two colors only!
I'm very sure you will agree with me, —
The flower-art is a pretty sphere, that suits
The genius of the modern Spaniard well.

ELEANOR.

He would not send an awkward bunch of flowers
To any lady, be she young or old;
Besides, it is a virtue to do well
Whate'er we undertake.

EVERARD.

'Tis very true;
A good rule, I suppose: so thinks, perchance,
The matador who gashes at the bull.

ELEANOR.

That is a sudden leap from flowers, señor.

EVERARD.

Precisely so; just as the Spanish taste
Is hovering between the gay and cruel,
Effeminacy and barbarity.

[*He rises up.*

Will you not go to see the play to-night?

ELEANOR.

Yes: aunt, I think, has so arranged for us.

EVERARD.

Then I may do myself, perhaps, the pleasure
To join your party, if you will allow.

ELEANOR.

We shall be happy of your company.

[*He goes out.*

ELEANOR.

There is some truth in what he says, I fear;
And yet he passes sentence on them all.
I think he is unjust, — he is unfair.

[*She rises, and goes out.*

SCENE III.

Night. Secret meeting of Spanish Liberals. Groups in close conversation.

FIRST SPANIARD.

You have confidence, you say, in Alancia?

SECOND SPANIARD.

Entire confidence. I don't expect him to do much of the work: he's not had the training for it; it isn't his style. But it's a great thing to have the name of a high-toned young nobleman on our list.

FIRST SPANIARD.

Yes: the sound goes a great way with the gaping crowd.

SECOND SPANIARD.

'Tis something more than sound: it is a power with a certain set of honest Conservatives, who are very much afraid we are hot-headed fools.

FIRST SPANIARD.

You don't think he'll flinch?

SECOND SPANIARD.

Not a bit of it.

THIRD SPANIARD.

He has drawn in some of the young blood already.

FIRST SPANIARD.

I am afraid of them all: every one may turn out a mal sujeto.

SECOND SPANIARD.

Never you fear; I am more afraid of the rabble below us.

FIRST SPANIARD.

What do you think of Valdegamas' speech?

SECOND SPANIARD.

I think we hissed him pretty well.

FIRST SPANIARD.

Still, it will be considered a great success, you may depend upon it: the papers call the speech "very sublime."

SECOND SPANIARD.

Yes, yes: it *was* sublime where he rose to his climax about the costliness of republics, and standing armies being the cheapest machinery of government. There was a Teutonic fire in his eye, and his head was in the clouds, after the most wrapt German fashion.

FIRST SPANIARD.

It is a pity he did not stay in Berlin.

SECOND SPANIARD.

The Government is pretty hard up, when it sends for such a scatter-brained foreign minister to help uphold its policy.

FIRST SPANIARD.

Don't be too confident.

SECOND SPANIARD.

I can't think he'll do us a bit of harm.

SCENE IV.

In the house of SIR HENRY IVERTON. SIR HENRY *with* ELEANOR *in his despacho.*

SIR HENRY (*taking up a card*).

What's this? The duke has left another card!
Three times he's been here in the last two weeks.
What can he want of me?

ELEANOR.

The duke! what duke?

SIR HENRY.

Why, that young Manuel de Alancia.
Can't be that he has sense enough to see
That you are prettier than these silly girls,
Who use their black eyes so? eh, Eleanor?

ELEANOR.

Me, uncle! it is you he comes to see,
Is't not? Have you forgotten how he looked
At your old English hunting-dress one day;
And how he took the rifle down, and spear,
And asked about the game, and said, — while he
Was smoothing down the fur upon your cap, —
Our England must be sure a merry place?

SIR HENRY.

Yes, yes: I do remember, so he did:
He had the wit to like it, say you, then?
'Tis more than could be often said of them,
These little-waisted Spaniards here in town.
Where's Everard of late? he's not been in?

ELEANOR.

Yes: he was here on Sunday night, at tea.

SIR HENRY.

You did not drive him off with all your fun,
Your foolery, among those Spanish girls?

ELEANOR.

Him, uncle? no: he's not so shy as that.
He teased the little señoritas, too,
Far more than they could trouble him.

SIR HENRY.

And you?
He does not tease you, Eleanor?

ELEANOR.

Me? no, sir;
Because he's learned that I cannot be teased.

[*She turns to go out.*

SIR HENRY.

Eleanor, stay, and listen now to me.
I wish to speak to you; sit down awhile,
There's no one here to interrupt us now.
Eleanor, I have very often wished
That Everard might one day be your husband.
This morning, from some words he dropt to me,
I understood his feelings plain enough;
Are you surprised, my girl?

ELEANOR.

Ye—s, uncle; no:
For I have sometimes thought you wished for this,
And yet I did not think so in my heart.

SIR HENRY.

And, pray, why not?

ELEANOR.

He does not love me, first.

SIR HENRY.

Not love you? well, I looked to hear you say
You loved not him. Ha, ha! Upon my word,
That is a crotchet that I never thought of.

ELEANOR.

He knows not how to love, — he knows not how.

SIR HENRY.

Do you not hear, my child? He seeks your hand;
You are not rich, — what should it be but love?

ELEANOR.

He thinks, perhaps, I'll make a prudent wife.

SIR HENRY.

Ah! like you not his wooing of you, then?
He looks not ill to me in face nor form.

ELEANOR.

He does not please me.

SIR HENRY.

Child, what would you like?
You'd have him "put himself," then, "at your feet,"
Just like the Spanish dandies; ha! is't so?

I warrant ye, I warrant ye, my girl,
He would be there in truth, long while before
Your sentimental dons, who talk so fine.

ELEANOR.

Good! uncle; I should like to see him there.
He's far too much in love with his own self,
To bend so low as that.

SIR HENRY.

Be serious, child:
I'm not in mood for jokes.

ELEANOR.

'Twas you begun it.

SIR HENRY.

Come, come, come, —

ELEANOR (*interrupting him*).

He has no faith in aught that's good or high,
Dear uncle; he's a sneerer at all things;
He has no faith excepting in himself, —
In his own self-advancement and career.

SIR HENRY.

You wrong him, Eleanor: that is his way.

ELEANOR.

His way!

SIR HENRY.

Hush! listen now to what I say:
Do you not think I wish your happiness?
Do you believe that I would have you wed
This man, or any other under heaven,
Unless I thought it for your good, my child?
I am not young; I cannot always live,
And Everard's an honest gentleman;
More, he has talents which will fit him for
Some high and honorable career at home.
He has a fortune not to be despised,
For I have nothing but my salary;
Heaven knows I'd gladly leave my all to you,
But it is little. Do you not believe
Your mother's favorite brother has at heart
The interest of her child? Do you not think
I love you, Eleanor, her orphan child?

ELEANOR (*bursting into tears*).

Forgive me, uncle, I have not deserved
Your kindness ever; no, forgive me, uncle,
I did not doubt your love, — not that, not that.

SIR HENRY (*aside*).

Just like her mother now, she is, the girl;
And yet, somehow, I did not use to mind
Her tears so much, for they came oftener.

[*To* ELEANOR.

Well, well, my child; some other time, perhaps,
We'll talk this matter over. Never mind,

You are my own good girl; come, brighten up.
Come, play a game of chess; ring for some wood, —
The room is cold; we'll have a blazing fire, —
Yes, we'll not shiver like these Spanish folks,
And crouch around a pan of smutty coals.

[*Enter* SERVANT.

SERVANT.

A gentleman waits, sir.

SIR HENRY.

Let him come up.

[ELEANOR *slips out, and goes into her aunt's boudoir adjoining.* LADY IVERTON *sits there.*

SCENE V.

LADY IVERTON *and* ELEANOR.

LADY IVERTON.

Why, Eleanor, I've wondered where you were.
You're looking pale: in truth, we're all worn out
With such late hours as we have had this week.

ELEANOR.

I? I am very well. What have you there?
What are you reading, aunt?

LADY IVERTON.

Oh! nothing new.

[*She lays down her book.*

Eleanor, now I think of it, — I wish
To warn you early, how you do receive
Attentions from the Spaniards at this court.

ELEANOR.

What mean you, aunt?

LADY IVERTON.

Why, there can be no harm
If they admire you, for it gives *éclat*
To your position, and one would not wish
That you should be without such compliment;
Yet you must not forget the gossiping
About this idle court: besides, you know
You would not ever think to marry here.
I heard some gossip from the servants' hall
This very afternoon; I heard your name.

ELEANOR (*rising up pale*).

What dared they say?

LADY IVERTON.

Why, nothing dreadful, child.
They said Don Manuel de Alancia
Was mad in love with you. I know, myself,
The court is talking of the handsome duke;
Some think you favor him, and some do not.

[ELEANOR *draws a long breath; then, flushing deep, she goes and stirs the fire. After musing awhile, she turns.*

ELEANOR.

And uncle, — does he know of all this gossip?

LADY IVERTON.

No, no: I have not dared to tell him yet.

ELEANOR.

Dear aunt, you're not afraid that I shall lose
My self-respect?

LADY IVERTON.

Oh, no: I only meant
To caution you to be upon your guard.

ELEANOR (*stands looking into the fire sometime; then turns, and takes a candle*).

Aunt, I'm so wearied with these many hours
Of dissipation, that I'll say good-night.

LADY IVERTON.

You're going now? So must I soon; good-night.

[*Exit* ELEANOR.

LADY IVERTON.

I think that I have put a stop to it;
There's nothing she so hates as vulgar gossip.
It is vexatious that a girl like her,
With nothing but her beauty in her favor,
Should take the laurels all away from me.

SCENE VI.

ELEANOR *in her chamber, smiling to herself.*

He's "mad in love," he's "mad in love," they say;
And yet I never gave him word nor look:
They dare not say I am in love with him.
'Tis true, one day, when I looked quickly up,
And saw him gazing so on me, I blushed;
And, when he spoke, I stammered a reply, —
But what was that?
I am forgetting all
That uncle said to me of Everard.
Everard! I cared not if he came or went;
But now he's hateful to me; hateful now.
Why do I think so much about this Spaniard?
And *do* I care for him? I always said
I did not value beauty; and I laughed
To see the fancy, 'mong the girls at school,
For some mustachioed, lisping foreigner.
I had no faith in southern passion then;
But am I changed so much in these few weeks?
Or is he different from common men?
It is not what he says, or what he does:
There is a charm around when he is near;
All things seem high, romantic, beautiful.
I wonder, when I hear the Spanish girls
Bant'ring at ease with him on every theme,
They are not more abashed before his gaze,

His noble taste, his pride, his chivalry.
He sees them, after all, with Spanish eyes.
He is a Spaniard: what is he to me?
A Roman Catholic, — he looks at life
From quite another view, I fear, than I.
Poor, foolish girl, he cannot be for thee!
And uncle, — he'd despise me if he thought
I scorned his friend, to love a Spanish *duke*.

[*She muses awhile.*

And there's poor Milverton, I left at home;
He's wiser than Alancia, I doubt not.
He lent me books; he taught me German, too:
Yes, he knew every thing that's worth the knowing;
And yet, somehow, — 'tis strange, — I did not wish,
When he went out, he would come back again.
He had the poetry of every age
Upon his tongue; but this man's very life
Is flowing over with his being's music:
I feel it, and I know not what it is.
I do suppose he loved me, — Milverton;
He praised sincerely every thing I did,
But I was quite content to rest me there:
I did not long, as with Alancia,
To go for ever on, and yearn to make
The good in me more lovely in his eyes.

Ah me! where is to be the end, — the end?
Why did I ever come to this strange land?
Why did I go away, and leave my home,

The little quiet lanes? the holly-boughs
They hung for Christmas, when I said good-by.
The roses there are innocent and fresh,
And sweeter than exotics. Is this love
A gay exotic for the northern heart,
That early blooms — and fades away — and dies?
Oh, mother! resting in the churchyard there,
Thou little dream'st thy daughter is ensnared
In all the pitfalls of a far-off land!
Thy quiet Eleanor, who cared for naught
But to be sitting all the day with thee,
Or wandering for the wild anemones,
To make thy pale face smile when thou wast sick,
And never wearied her poor head with love.

[*She throws herself into a chair. Suddenly she starts up.*

What if he should be trifling with my heart?
O heaven, that I should come to this, — to this!
Take me away from this deceitful land.
No, no: I will not think so low of him.
What shall I do then? Shall I suffer him
To meet me everywhere, and by-and-by,
In cool words, say I cannot see him more?

[*She weeps. Throws herself in the chair again.*

Mother! teach me, I pray, the way to go;
I'm lost, bewildered in this dangerous maze.

[*She sits a long time thinking, and at length falls asleep. She wakes, half dreaming.*

I thought I saw Alancia! He wore
One of my English roses on his breast.

He said, "We will live there: the air is sweet;
The northern sky burns not with feverish heat,
But gloweth deep and pure as thy blue eye;
The Virgin, too, will watch us from on high,—
Thou wilt not scorn her heavenly ministry."

Ah! 'twas a dream.

[*She rises, and goes to her sleeping room.*

SCENE VII.

The DUKE OF ALANCIA *and* DON FERMIN MORALES *in a by-street, talking.*

DON FERMIN.

Bravo, my man! you're getting in pretty deep.

ALANCIA.

Tut, boy! these things are not to be spoken of by daylight.

DON FERMIN.

Why, my fine fellow, is that the kind of lover you make?

ALANCIA.

Lover? I was not talking about love, you scamp.

DON FERMIN.

I *was;* and I was in hopes it had taken the wind out of your Liberal sails. Come, why don't you speak? The truth is, when a man's in love, he may as well throw up other matters.

ALANCIA.

I never told you I was in love.

DON FERMIN.

That was not at all necessary. Vamos! you've given up this crazy scheme, of course; you'll have love-songs to write, — you can't do both.

You've thrown up your politics, of course?

ALANCIA.

No, señor.

DON FERMIN.

Do you mean to say you are going on with this mad project.

ALANCIA.

Si, señor.

DON FERMIN.

You can't mend a broken dish.

ALANCIA.

There is a new kind of cement.

DON FERMIN.

What is it?

ALANCIA.

Liberty.

DON FERMIN.

It will be a cracked dish after all. It will fall apart while you are doing it, and gash your fingers.

ALANCIA.

Then some one else will take it up, and try again.

DON FERMIN.

Oh, Don Quijote Valoroso!
Worthy of thy Dulcinea del Toboso.

ALANCIA.

Fermin, let us understand each other. I have sworn to do my duty by my country; it is of no use to reason with me: God only knows what will be the end. Farewell.

[ALANCIA *rushes away, talking to himself.*

It is foolish trying to deceive him or myself: I *am* in love. Life is too sweet for me to wish to die just now. When I first came home, I held it cheaper; I was sick of the littleness of the world; I thought I should like to do something great, and quit it. Now it seems to me that *love* is the greatest thing in the world, yet I believe I am no worse patriot; I cannot, I would not, recede from the path I have taken.

SCENE VIII.

In the house of Doña Maria de Alancia. Doña Maria *and the duke, her son.*

DOÑA MARIA.

My son, why art thou sitting there so dull?
I'd rather thou wouldst write thy poetry,
Than idle all the afternoon away.
Come, cheer thee up, and let us go and see
The people on the Prado, this fine day;
Shame, to be staying in the house at spring!
Send for thy horse; thou art too handsome far
To grope for ever in these narrow streets.
The queen, too, will be sweeping up and down
Between the thronging line of carriages;
Ah, how they will be pressing on the walk!
And all in gala such a pleasant day.
The Countess Anita is always there
At four o'clock; she knows the difference
Between such figure as thou carriest
Upon thy horse, and others riding there.

[Alancia *shrugs his shoulders.*

Ah! thou art thinking of the English girl.

ALANCIA.

Dear mother, I have other things to do, —
Have other things than love to think of now.

DOÑA MARIA.

Then wherefore be so foolish as to vex
Thy noble soul about this foreigner?
An alien to thy race, thy tongue, thy faith, —
Believe thy mother, she is strange and cold
And passionless. I watched her yesternight:
There was no passion in her looks at thee.

ALANCIA (*impatiently*).

Thou knowest naught about it, mother. Hist!

DOÑA MARIA.

And I was glad; I knew thou could'st not waste
Thy heart upon this fair, cold creature long,
When there are other handsome eyes in Spain,
Eager to answer back unto thine own.

ALANCIA.

Answer before I ask it, mother mine.

DOÑA MARIA.

And what of that, my son; and what of that?
'Tis better than a false and moveless face,
That throws its snares around thee, one by one,
And coldly smiles and smiles, untouched itself.

ALANCIA.

Stop, mother, if thou mean'st the young Inglesa.

DOÑA MARIA.

Listen, my son, for am I not thy mother?
Thou art a foolish boy. What is her faith?
Think thou of that.

[*Crossing herself.*

Jesus! she owneth not
The blessed Virgin Mother's intercession:
She sitteth on a cushioned seat at church,
And readeth from her book: and that is all
Her worship of the Crucified, my son.

ALANCIA.

Mother, she loves to go unto our church.

DOÑA MARIA.

She looketh with a stranger's curious eye
Upon the blessed saints that stand about,
To count the cunning carvings in their robes.
'Tis madness in thee, son; yes, madness, boy!

ALANCIA.

Mother, thou'rt cruel! Talk not to me thus:
Thou know'st not how I love this English girl.

DOÑA MARIA.

But think; her rank, — how small compared with thine.
We're poor, but not in name or blood, I trust.
Thy verses, too; it pleased me not at first
To see thee moping with thy pen and ink, —

It was not like thy father (now in peace,
With all the blessed saints in Paradise),
Although thou lack'st not spirit ever: no, —
But, I confess, thy pen will make thee soon
The darling of the court.

ALANCIA.

Not of the court, —
The court, my mother; that were small, indeed;
I would belong to Spain, be loved of Spain.

DOÑA MARIA.

And that thou shalt, and that thou shalt, my son.
And Spain shall ring, —

ALANCIA.

I care not for it all.
Mother, be true, and answer me. Did'st wed
My father, now, because he was a duke?
He saw thee in thy Andalusian home;
Thou thought'st he was a poor young soldier lad:
He won thy heart before thou knew'st his name;
Did'st love him more, because he proved a duke?

DOÑA MARIA (*with tears in her eyes*).

He had a look that spoke a courtly soul.

ALANCIA.

And so hath she, my mother, — so hath she.
Oh, she is beautiful! but 'tis her soul, —

It is her soul I love. For she is pure
And innocent and maidenly as they, —
The lovely ladies were, of whom we read
In olden books, who kept all harm away
By their sweet presence, and commanding looks.
And she has courage, too, and noble fire:
If she could know that I were called by heaven
Unto some new crusade (ah! I *am* called),
She'd bid me go with lofty, kindling eye
(Provided she did love me); with her look
Upon my heart indelibly impressed,
I'd conquer whatsoe'er she bade me meet.
Rememb'rest not, my mother, how the knights,
Who never were disloyal to their faith,
Did love their foreign ladies o'er the sea?

DOÑA MARIA.

They were not cold and learned Protestants.

ALANCIA.

Nay, mother, worse than Protestants, indeed.
Did not young Tancred love the Saracen
Clorinda, heretic and infidel?

DOÑA MARIA.

I care not for thy rusty knights, my son;
Thou'rt ever talking of thy heroes, boy;
I pray thee be a hero: fling aside
The evil spell that spoils thy youth and strength,

And marry Anita. Thou wilt get well
Beneath her little velvet eyes ; and, when
Thou art our poet, Spain will love thee more,
Because that thou hast wed in thine own land.

ALANCIA.

I cannot marry her, — not for the world.
Mother, if thou did'st know how I do love
This English lady, thou would'st rather pray, —
Thou would'st fall down before her sacred feet,
And pray that she would smile upon thy son.
Thou would'st be grateful to the saints, indeed,
Should they so bless thy threshold as to bring
Such heavenly guest unto thy house and home.

DOÑA MARIA.

Thou ravest now, my son ; be calm, be calm.

ALANCIA.

No, no : it is because thou'lt not believe.
When by her side, my mother, I am calm
And self-possessed, and I love all things, too ;
And if she chances happily to praise
What I have done, I can do more ; ay, more,
And better too. Sweet mother, I could write
So that the world should listen to me long,
With my dear northern lady ever near
To fire me with her lofty, guiding thought,
And warm me with her tender eyes.

Hast marked
How they do change from blue to grey, so like
The sky of summer, at the glow of noon,
Then, in the gentle sombreness of night?
If I were but Murillo, I would paint
The flakes of gold that play around her hair
So well, thou would'st believe that thou could'st see
The glory of the Virgin on her head.
Dost thou remember holy Mary's gaze,
As she is floating there among the clouds, —
The look of sweet surprise and earnestness?
Just so she looketh up inquiringly
When I am telling her of things that please,
And smiles on me in lovely innocence.

DOÑA MARIA.

Dost thou believe she loves thee?

ALANCIA (*coloring*).

What of that?
I was not speaking of her love for me,
But mine for her.

DOÑA MARIA.

Thou hast far too much pride,
I deem, my son, to hear them say at court,
Don Manuel, the duke, is mad in love
With yon Inglesa; and doth let her sport
With him, and show to all the gaping world,
How she hath got a handsome gentleman, —

Of birth the noblest in the kingdom, too,
Admired of ladies, wedded or unwed,—
Down underneath her careless, haughty feet.

ALANCIA.

Hush, mother! name Elena not, I say,
With those poor butterflies that conquer hearts:
She is no trifler. And for all the town
I care not; let them whisper as they choose:
What can they say, except that I do love?
And I am proud of that.

DOÑA MARIA.

E'en if she's cold?

ALANCIA (*springing up*).

She hath too much of woman's dignity
To open wide her pure and noble heart,
And shew its workings unto any man,
At each emotion which doth stir her breast;
She is not like the Andalusian maids.

DOÑA MARIA.

Dost thou mean me, my son? I never gave
My heart unto thy father till he asked.

ALANCIA.

No, no: forgive me, mother, for my words.
But will thou not then wait awhile before

Thou call'st her cold? till I have told her all?

[*He walks up and down the room; talks to himself.*

No, no: it is a shadowy hope, — a dream.
Fool, fool am I! it is her lovely way:
It meaneth nothing; she is always so.
Heavens, mother! maybe thou art in the right.
No, she hath not a cold heart, — thou art wrong:
But whether she doth care for thy poor son —

[*He turns towards his mother.*

Mother, if it be true she will not hear
My suit; if it be true she does not love, —
I shall at least have one more thing to do
In this drear world, — to die for my poor country.

[*He darts out of the room.*

DOÑA MARIA (*following him*).

Hear, Manuel, but a word, — a word, my son.
He's gone; what does he mean? O Manuel!

[*Exit.*

PART III.

SCENE I.

The Buen Retiro. An early hour, before the arrival of the crowd.
ELEANOR *and her maid,* JUANA. *The former seated on a bench.*

ELEANOR.

Juana, go and bring a sprig of green, —
A branch of cedar from that little tree.

JUANA.

Carámba! Señorita, 'tis the queen's.

ELEANOR.

Oh, mind not that! the queen is very kind;
It is a pity that I should not have
One little sprig, to carry in my book
Away across the waters to my home.

JUANA.

Ay, little señorita, how you love
The precious book of dried and faded flowers!

I'll go and bring a pretty rose for you.
I knew the gardener, when he and I
Were living with a Spanish gentleman;
He had the care of all those handsome grounds,
And he would bring in flowers so beautiful,
And tie them up with many a ribbon fine,
For me to carry in to my señora.
Ah, madre mia, how he boasted then!

ELEANOR.

Well, well; thou wilt not get the flowers, I fear,
If thou dost stay so long and talk, Juana.

JUANA.

Bien; I'll go this instant, señorita.

[*She returns after some minutes.*

Look, look! carnations, roses, heliotropes.
I told him of my mistress, the Inglesa,
And how my señorita had a book,
With thousand flowers from every land on earth;
And he was mighty pleased, for "he could speak
The English," and he wondered I could not.
My faith, I don't believe he knows it much;
He called you "Mees," the way I call my cat.
See, see! he gave me these, and offered more.

ELEANOR (*smiles a little, and takes the flowers*).

Bravo, Juana! they are beautiful.

JUANA.

Hark, hark! Ah! would the señorita mind
If I should go through yonder little grove,
To see the engine pass along the plain?
I hear it coming now.

ELEANOR.

No; haste away.

[*She runs off.* ELEANOR *drops the flowers in her lap.*

Simple Juana, how I envy thee!
Thou art so pleased to see the noisy train, —
The only one, in truth, thy land can boast.
And many older ones than thou I've known
Run up the neighboring ledge to see it pass, —
The same delight in all their Spanish eyes.
And I — I sit and smile complacently,
Glad to escape the din of wiser lands.

[*She muses awhile.*

Why are we northerners so satisfied
Because we have advanced a step or more
In worldly lore? we're far enough behind,
It may be, in the searching eye of God.
And what if, as we're hurrying on so fast,
We do not see the pictures as we pass
Along the road of life, nor stop to sit
Beside some little purling stream, nor watch
With dreaming eyes the golden evening light.

[*She rises, smiles to herself, and walks to another part of the grounds, and sits down.*

SCENE II.

Don Fermin Morales *in another walk.*

DON FERMIN.

Ah! that is it; I have it; that is why
Alancia started off. I'll wager, now,
He saw the young Inglesa in the grounds.

[He goes off singing.

Ay, I love a pretty girl;
Wherefore, wherefore all this fuss?
Love is not a sullen churl,
All so solemn, serious.

Fa-la-la.

SCENE III.

Alancia *hurries up to* Eleanor, *salutes her, and throws himself down on the grass by her seat. She starts, and blushes.*

ALANCIA.

Pardon this boldness, — pardon me, I pray;
I have a word to speak to thee to-night.
I chanced to see thy figure through the trees:
I would not break the quiet of thy walk;
But can I wait? This life is far too short;
I cannot go, till I have told thee all.

I love thee, señorita; thou hast seen
How I am wholly thine in heart and soul.

[*She trembles, and tries to speak.*

Nay, do not think me rash, presumptuous;
I have no right, indeed, to speak to thee,
Except the right which every loyal heart
Doth have to tell its homage and its love.

ELEANOR (*with trembling voice*).

Thou must not speak of this, Alancia;
I cannot hear it: I must forfeit all
Thy kindness and thy friendship, if thou dost.

[*She starts to go.*

ALANCIA.

Stay; I'll do all thou bidst, if thou wilt stay.

ELEANOR (*she sits down trembling*).

I thank thee for thy love: it is in vain
For thee to waste thy noble heart on me.
Go find another of thy race and tongue,
Who will reward thee better far than I.

ALANCIA.

Elena!

ELEANOR.

Go write thy book, and charm the listening world;
Nor let a fancy for the English girl
Bedim the genius which should keep itself
All bright for thy own land, for fame, for glory.

ALANCIA.

Elena, thou can'st know me not if thou
Dost think that I can take my pen again,
My paltry pen, and write of love and truth
As once of old, when I had not seen thee.

ELEANOR.

Then I have robbed thee of thy happiness, —
Have spoiled the honors which should one day fall
Upon thy head, to give thee nothing back.

ALANCIA.

Thou sayst that thou can'st give me — nothing — back?
Thou hast then said it. 'Twas a reckless dream;
I'll trouble thee no more, if it be so.
Farewell, Elena! may the saints protect thee!

[*He springs up quickly, and starts away.*

ELEANOR (*hurriedly*).

Alancia, come back; I did not say, —
Thou did'st not understand my words aright.

[*He turns.*

ALANCIA.

It is thy kindness; yes, I know, indeed,
That thou would'st have me feel thou art my friend.
I thank thee — thou art good — for all the hours,
The blessed hours, which I have spent with thee.
I was an idle wanderer on the earth:

Since I knew thee, I have looked into heaven.
But no, — I cannot take thy kindness now.

ELEANOR.

I said I could not give thee happiness,
If I were kind, should I have called thee back?

[*He watches her fixedly.*

If thou wast happy, I — I was not sad;
If thou art sad, I am not gay as once;
If thou hast dashed away a pleasant dream,
So then have I: it is not thou alone.

[*She blushes deeply.*

If thou hast given away thy heart, then I —
Shall not forget thee soon, Alancia.

[*He seizes her hand, and kisses it.*

Be calm, be calm, Alancia, I pray.
'Tis wrong: but yet I could not have thee deem
That all the English maidens are so cold.
Did'st thou not ever think I cared for thee?

[*He darts forward.*

No, no: be still, or I shall run from thee.

ALANCIA (*throwing himself again on the grass by her seat*).

I thought so oft, and went from thee at times
As joyous as the wind; but when I saw
Thee moving 'mong the chilly diplomats,
So fair and stately, then I feared that thou
Had'st little place for me within thy heart;
And early left the sick'ning rooms at night,

Impatient at thy courteous smiles on them,
And weary of the heartlessness around.

ELEANOR.

My *courteous* smiles, thou own'st; was I to thee
Then *courteous* only, when we talked so long,
One night, the red-mustachioed Austrian count,
With all his stars and crosses, whispered sly;
And the old Major Domo bustled round,
With looks at thee which plainly showed he thought
Thou should'st be dancing in the royal set?
Was I too eager then to leave thy side,
And promenade with those bedizened men, —
Those self-sufficient dignitaries there?

ALANCIA.

No, no: thou wast too good, — too good, indeed;
But I would have thee wholly to myself.

ELEANOR.

Ah! thou must speak no more such words to me;
They are the first, they are the last for us.
Our homes are wide apart; a different faith
Is mine from thine. Thy mother, too, confess,
Would weep to see her only son beloved
Of me, a foreigner and Protestant.
Thy country's laws forbid such love in truth;
The dear old bishop, Cardinal of Spain, —
Whom I do reverence as much as thou, —
Could not pronounce a blessing on our heads.

ALANCIA.

So be it: they cannot divide our hearts,
And Spain is not the only land on earth.

ELEANOR.

But more: my uncle would be much displeased
To hear thy words; he does not love thy land.
He hopes to see me wed some Englishman,
Who'd give to his old age companionship,
And me protection when he is no more.
Dost thou not know I am an orphan girl?

ALANCIA.

By heaven! thou shalt not want protection then.

ELEANOR.

That he has loved me since my father died,
With all a parent's pride and tenderness?
That I have only what he gives to me,
Showering his kindnesses upon my head,
With not a harsh demand in payment yet?
And shall I slight his wishes, then? his first?
No, no: I do deceive him now, — yes, now,
While I am talking here with thee. Away,
Away, I pray thee, — if thou — lovest me.

[*They hear* JUANA *returning through the trees. He seizes her hand, kisses it, and disappears.* ELEANOR *and* JUANA *return home.*

ALANCIA (*in another part of the grounds*).

Ah! what are lands and friends, religions, — all?
Dear heavens! she loveth me. She said it not, —
Those very words; but how she called me back!
"Alancia," she softly said: my name
Rang out so sweet and silvery, that ev'n now
It seems not like reality to me,
But far away, as if 'twere in my sleep.
Is it an omen dim that tells us we
Shall see each other henceforth but in dreams,
Where we shall talk together of our joy,
And wake up sudden to the dreadful day?
No, no: she loves me. Ah! the tears that came
In her sweet eyes. Most happy man thou art,
That thou could'st bring such happy tears as those, —
So few, so rare, so precious: not of grief.
Yes, let the fates do what they will to me,
They cannot wipe those glistening drops away,
Nor lay their fingers on those blushes warm,
And make them cold.
My mother, thou wast wrong,
Who thought'st thy foolish son could not be loved:
Elena was not cold: I told thee so.
Ah! whither am I going? here, again,
I see the very spot she left.
[*He stands and gazes at it.*
How lovely is the day! The Spring has come:
It is a paradise among these trees,
All young and tender; and the air is full

Of murmuring sounds from every living thing.
Not gay is it, nor melancholy music;
It meets the fever of my heart, subdues
And stills it all to lovely harmony.
But hark! they come; I hear the rushing tide
That pours adown the stately Alcala.
Ah! let them walk, poor souls, where'er they please,
They cannot know what makes this spot so sweet.

[*He looks once more at the seat, and hurries away.*

SCENE IV.

ALANCIA *standing in his patio, musing. Night.*

These noble patriots shall have my name and sympathies and influence, what little it is; and, if they fail, I will take the risks with them.

But as for the work itself, I cannot do it. I have no head for it: I won't say heart for it; for if ever I felt as if I could go through fire and water to do my duty, it is now that I have got the love of Elena Manton. But these intrigues, in the way of glory, are not inspiring. O love, love, love!

[*A dark* FIGURE *looks in at the gate, and speaks in a whisper.*

FIGURE.

Alancia, we're in pretty deep.

ALANCIA.

How are things going on?

FIGURE.

Bellamente! bellamente!

ALANCIA.

Quevedo, I'm no party man, no politician; but I love my country, and I can keep my word.

[*The* FIGURE *vanishes.* ALANCIA *goes in.*

SCENE V.

In the house of SIR HENRY IVERTON. SIR HENRY *and* LADY IVERTON.

SIR HENRY.

What think you, wife, of what I said to you
Concerning Everard and Eleanor?

LADY IVERTON.

I think with you; if Everard, as you say,
Has really asked to marry Eleanor,
'Twill not be wise to lose such overtures.
She's old enough to wed; we cannot hope
To make a splendid union for her ever.
She has no fortune of her own, no home,

And Everard's fit match enough for her:
Why should she not be married shortly, too?

SIR HENRY.

She has a home as long as I have one:
That is not why I speak; I should be loth
To see her leave my roof. A gentle girl,
And good and lovely is she: 'twill be hard
To hear no more her footsteps in the house;
She never gave me aught but pleasure yet.

LADY IVERTON.

Of course, of course; she's welcome to stay here:
I never yet did treat her otherwise.
But she must sometime marry, that is all;
And she will do as well as she can hope,
In taking Everard.

SIR HENRY.

What is't you mean?
I've told you, wife, a thousand times, that he, —
This Everard you patronize so much, —
Is not my secretary, but my friend.
"Fit match enough"! think you I'm turning off
My sister's orphan child unto a man
That's "good enough"? I would far rather keep
The little girl by me, unwooed for ever,
Than give her to a man I do not prize,
Because the world says women must be wed.

LADY IVERTON.

Well, well: he's talented, I do suppose,
Though I myself have never fancied him.

SIR HENRY.

Fancy! he's not a fancy man, forsooth;
If so, the women all would like him better.

LADY IVERTON.

Dear me! I cannot suit you at my best.
But, tell me, what think you of Eleanor?

SIR HENRY (*walking up and down*).

She? Why, she'll fret and fidget me, of course.
Where was there yet a woman who did not,
Whene'er a word was said to her about
A sensible, straightforward gentleman?

LADY IVERTON.

But she is dutiful; she will not think
Of setting up her will against your own.
Besides, you are her lawful guardian.

SIR HENRY.

There is the thing: I cannot bear to force her,
For she has ever done my slightest bidding.

LADY IVERTON (*eyeing him closely*).

You know about Alancia, I suppose?

SIR HENRY.

I know of nothing good or bad of him.

LADY IVERTON.

Why, that he is in love with Eleanor.

SIR HENRY.

If you keep open ears each time they say
A Spaniard is in love, you must have room
For little else.

LADY IVERTON.

It is no false report.

SIR HENRY.

How do you know?

LADY IVERTON.

I think she likes him, too.
It may be I am wrong.

SIR HENRY.

By George! is't so?
Fool was I not to look about me more;
You, wife, have got the sharper eyes, I grant.
I might have known her silly head was turned;
I never knew the girl to be so high,
So resolute, as when I spoke to her.

LADY IVERTON.

Ah! then you have already broached the subject?
What evening was it?

SIR HENRY (*walking up and down the room*).

So, she is in love
With one of these poor, miserable dogs, —
These dawdling hangers-on of royalty,
Without one honest pound to call their own;
Who blazon arms upon their equipage,
And ride about in gilded gaiety,
And kiss their sovereign's hand, to suck from it
The bounties which by right belong among
The loathsome wretches, crawling from their holes
Of mud and sand to till the soil, and raise
The oil and grape for these to fatten on.

LADY IVERTON.

Come, come: there's no use to berate the duke;
We'll stop it now, before it can go further.

SIR HENRY.

I could have born her opposition, too,
If 'twas her natural shrinking at our plans;
But that she should be carrying in her head
The look of this conceited foreigner,
And curl her little lip at such a man
As Everard, — it is too much, too much.
Who would have dreamed that she could be so weak, —

So like some forward miss, let loose from school!
She was so modest and so reasonable;
Her whole demeanor showed the quietness
And breeding of an English gentlewoman.
  I never feared to trust her anywhere:
Even in this Christian land, where they do keep
The younger women under lock and key;
And take them out, and marshall them abroad,
With swarthy dowager on either side,
Or grizzly old dueña, or a pair
Of chalky-facēd lackeys following on,
Lest some of these poor, sallow, spindling youths
Should stare or grimace at them in the streets, —
I did not fear to trust my Eleanor.
I'm disappointed in the girl. Heigh-ho!
These women are alike; yes, everywhere.
Comes there a single opportunity
For them to plunge their heads in foolish scrapes,
They're ready at the instant, though they may
Have had no previous lessons in the art.
'Tis instinct; they are all alike, — alike.
This pretty, little, blue-eyed girl of ours
Has had no opening for it heretofore:
I see she understands it, like the rest.

LADY IVERTON.

But where's the use of chafing so about it?
There's nothing, now, so terrible in this,
That young Alancia should make love to her.

SIR HENRY.

Madam, you said yourself she cared for him.

LADY IVERTON.

Well, what of that? You have a will, I trust.

SIR HENRY (*walking up and down*).

It is too much, — too much! Since I came here,
No single thing has troubled me so much.

LADY IVERTON.

Where is the use of wasting all these words?

SIR HENRY (*stopping suddenly*).

I will not have it: no; I'll be obeyed,
And she shall marry Everard; 'twill be
The wisest part that I can do for her:
She'll thank me some day in the end, I think,
When all this crazy nonsense is at rest,
And she's a happy and contented wife.

LADY IVERTON.

And you'll not speak to her about the duke?

SIR HENRY.

I shall repeat my wishes once again,
And let her know that I must be obeyed;
I will not treat her as a child quite yet,
Nor bar her in at once from this poor duke.

LADY IVERTON.

You'll have to speak to her with caution, though;
It will not do to break out in your fashion
With people who're in love: you'll have to use
A nicer treatment, if you'd gain your end.

SIR HENRY.

Madam, say you to her what pleases you,
And I will do what pleases me. Good night.

[*He goes out.*

SCENE VI.

LADY IVERTON *alone.* ELEANOR *enters, moves up and down absently, then seats herself at her work.*

LADY IVERTON.

Eleanor, all my prophecies were true:
Your uncle was offended when he heard
The stories which they tell about the duke.
He thinks you were deceiving him, I fear,
When, all the time he spoke to you that night,
You never mentioned young Alancia.

ELEANOR.

Dear aunt, pray tell me what have I to do
With all the gossip of this idle court?

LADY IVERTON.

I mentioned casually the thing to him,
Supposing that it must have reached his ears;
He burst into a passion when he heard
Your name so bandied round about the court.

ELEANOR.

Aunt, if we live in what we call the world, —
Made up of pleasure-seeking men and women,
Who find amusement in the watch they keep
Upon their neighbors, — we must pay for it,
And lend them our poor names with all the rest.

LADY IVERTON.

But 'tis not well to keep their tongues afloat;
And if the duke continues to pursue you,
I would advise you to discourage him.
You would not wish to keep him at your side,
Nor let them name you here the "blonde coquette,"
Like that young English girl a year ago?

ELEANOR.

The world shall never call me so, my aunt,
Till I have grown more skilful in the art.
What is this world you talk so much about?
Dear aunt, I pray you, have not all of us
A voice within, that tells us better far
What's right and what is wrong? And must we go
To some poor, little, shallow clique to learn
Their verdict on us every step we take?

LADY IVERTON (*aside*).

Upon my soul, I cannot really tell
Whether she loves or not; yet I *was* sure.

[*To* ELEANOR.

You're a strange girl, indeed; you will not hear
My arguments, although I could have sworn
They would have been the very ones to suit
With your fastidious and high ideas.
Your nicer sentiments, perhaps, you find
Are not so well for practice: eh, is't so?

ELEANOR.

Seeming, dear aunt, — is that the worst to fear?
Is that the greatest evil in the world?

[*To herself.*

If I were only sure of *being* right.

LADY IVERTON.

Alancia's friends will all bestir themselves.
They wish, even to the Queen of Spain herself,
That he should wed the Countess Anita.
They will not like to see him so engrossed,
Dancing attendance on a foreigner,
And you will bring upon yourself the spleen
And jealousy of all his relatives.
Beware of rousing Spanish enmity:
There'll be an end of all our quiet here.

ELEANOR.

Alancia is of age: I do not see
How 'tis that I am so responsible
To all his kith and kin for what he does.

LADY IVERTON (*aside*).

Pert little minx!

[*To* ELEANOR.

I think he means to marry Anita.
He likes to frighten his poor, silly mother,
And all his neighbors, by this dallying round:
Just as our own young lords are capering
Before they're fairly broken in the harness.
I do not think he'll find it very hard:
She's pretty, with her little tapering feet
And roguish eyes. He likes to dance with her,
But that is natural. You do not waltz;
I dare say, though, you find him very pleasant:
They say he has a wondrous flow of words.

I saw the prettiest bouquet of flowers,
When I called on the dowager, her mother:
I spoke admiringly of it to her.
She smiled, and said "'twas from Alancia:
He had such charming taste in all he did;
He was so elegant and gracioso."

[*A noise, as of visitors approaching, is heard.* ELEANOR *hastens out of the room, pale. The alarm proves false.*

LADY IVERTON (*remaining alone*).

I wonder how she liked the last I said.
Good-natured as she seems, she always had
A high, grand air, as if she'd put me down.
Just so her father came to Iverton
To ask her mother's hand, as if he were
My noble Lord of Buckingham himself,
And not a starving artist: yes, with all
Her graceful ways Sir Henry likes so much,
She has a deal of haughtiness in her.

[*She muses awhile.*

If Everard marries her, he'll take her back
Before the year is out, and I shall be
No longer put into the shade by her.

[*Exit* LADY IVERTON.

SCENE VII.

ELEANOR *alone.*

O heavens! is that cold woman in the right?
And did she know how she was stabbing me?
She saw the color flying from my face:
She did not see how my heart stopt at once.

[*Walking back and forth.*

He seeks amusement with me, so she thinks;
There is no man on earth shall dare to do it,

Though I have had the folly to be pleased,
And the insanity to love such man.

[She stops suddenly.

But, after all, why should I trust her gaze,
That never saw beyond the surface yet?
And doubt his earnest look, his simple words,
His truthful heart?

[She sobs convulsively.

But yet they're keen and sharp,
Those eyes of hers. Where is it I am going?
Into some dreadful cheat? 'tis false, 'tis false!
Here I am doubting now the words that came,—
Came from the sweetest heart that ever beat.
What if he gave a few poor flowers to her,—
To Anita? Could I not spare her them,
When every throb of his dear, faithful breast
Is mine, if aught upon the earth be true?

[She wipes her tears.

God save me this belief alone, though I
Should never, never see him more!
'Tis sweet
To find that we are not deceived, where'er
This weary life may lead our sorrowing steps.

[She dresses, and goes out for a walk.

PART IV.

SCENE I.

At the Opera House. ELEANOR *in the box of an old* SPANISH LADY. *Several* GENTLEMEN *are there.* "*La Favorita*" *is the play.*

SPANISH LADY.

What think you, caballeros, of the part?
Sortero plays it bravely.

FIRST GENTLEMAN.

Ay, señora.

SECOND GENTLEMAN.

Yes, he's a rare muchacho: he will do
His own love-making hotly, I suspect.

THIRD GENTLEMAN.

Cuerpo de mi! what jealousy is that.

FIRST GENTLEMAN (*turning to* ELEANOR).

Fair señorita, are you pleased to-night?

ELEANOR.

Ah, yes: the music is most beautiful;
The airs have grown to be my favorites.

The play is rightly named; think you not so?

[*Turning to* ALANCIA, *who sits abstracted among them.*

ALANCIA.

Your pardon, señorita: did you speak?

ELEANOR (*with voice slightly trembling*).

Do you not think this play is rightly named?
It has a fascination of its own,
Like some sweet flower or shell, I know not why.

ALANCIA.

Yes, all the music is most beautiful.

SPANISH LADY.

Yet I for one, by half, would rather see
Lucrezia, with a dagger in her eyes;
Or Semiramide upon her throne.
How rich the show, how gay, magnificent!
There was no end, — no end to all the blaze,
The splendor, when the queen was here to see it.

[*The* GENTLEMEN *leave the box by degrees.* ALANCIA *remains. The Señora falls asleep.*

ALANCIA (*approaching* ELEANOR).

Elena, have you then forgotten all?
And was it but a dream I had of you,
The other morn in the Retiro's walks?
Do you repent of what you said to me?
Am I no more to you than these, to-night?

ELEANOR.

No: I have not forgot, Alancia;
I would I had. No, no, Alancia:
I would not lose the memory of that hour,
If I could gain my peace all back again.
But I am weary of these doubts and fears,
These everlasting reasonings with my heart.

ALANCIA.

Why speakest thou of *reason?* How is that?
I do not reason when I think of thee.

ELEANOR.

I do not reason if I love or not;
But is it right to play a daily cheat,
And let my rightful guardians believe
I think no more of thee than half the men
Who hold my fan a moment gracefully,
And say their little nothings, and depart?
Is this the way to treat my honored uncle?
No: I must tell him all, e'en though we part.

ALANCIA.

Pray, what has he to dò with it, Elena?

ELEANOR.

Ah! much indeed, my friend; ah! much indeed.

ALANCIA.

Thou knowest what is right, as well as he;
The saints and angels keep thee company:
Thou can'st not even think of what is wrong.

ELEANOR (*after resting her head some time on her hand*).

I had strange thoughts of thee the other night:
'Twas but a moment. Oh! I doubted thee;
I will not tell thee why it was, — 'tis gone.

ALANCIA.

What was it?

ELEANOR.

Never mind it now. I thought
That thou wast not, perhaps, in earnest with me.
I've heard that southern passion is a thing
That comes, and goes as quickly as it came.

ALANCIA.

Now cursed be fate that gave me being here!
I know thou seest only in my love
The frothy foaming of hot Spanish blood,
Like this Italian raving here to-night;

Thou dost not understand the Spanish soul,
If thou dost think 'tis made to flash out fire
At every touch, like yonder foreigner.

ELEANOR (*softly*).

Be thou not angry now, Alancia;
Why should I doubt, unless I loved thee so?
[*He looks earnestly at her.*
I am a stranger, of a far-off land;
Our ways, our thoughts, are not like those of Spain.
Thou hast a lovely friend in Anita.

ALANCIA.

Am I so poor of soul, then, in thine eyes,
That thou must speak to me of her, Elena?

ELEANOR.

Forgive; I did not mean to wound: but yet
I know — I know she is thy mother's choice.

ALANCIA.

Elena, she, compared with thee, is like
The russet sunflower — standing all the hours,
Amid the glare of day's enticing look,
Before the gaze of every traveller —
Beside the lovely rose that sits beneath
Its modest covering of tender green,
And waiteth to be sought, and breatheth o'er
Its happy finder purest fragrance sweet.

ELEANOR (*blushing*).

Thou art a poet, Manuel: 'tis the play
Of thine own fancies, throwing round me now
The graces which thou dost believe are mine.
May'st thou not waken some day from thy dream,
And see with other eyes thy poor Inglesa?

ALANCIA.

Elena, would that I had now the power
To speak in common, plainest phrase of speech;
Like some poor, dullard peasant, who at least
Can say unto his mistress that he loves,
And end it there, since haply she believes.
The poet's tongue: ah! I could tear it out,
If I am talking with it pretty lies, —
Yes, lovely lies, to cheat myself and thee.

ELEANOR.

Nay, nay, dear friend, thou must not fling away
Thy greatest glory in Elena's eyes:
She would not have thee seem like other men.
If thou dost value not thy golden key,
Unlocking all the secrets of the world,
Then will Elena wear it on her heart,
Till in some moment she may please thee more,
And thou wilt take it back, and charm her still.

ALANCIA.

Thou pleasest me too well, thou little one.

ELEANOR.

I'll tell thee why I was so jealous, then:
Thou sent'st some flowers to Anita, didst not?

ALANCIA.

Dear heart, her mother begged the flowers of me
One morning, as I met her in the street,
The little countess walking by her side:
I could no less than say that they were hers.

ELEANOR (*smiling*).

Forgive me, if I question thee too hard;
This is a land, thou knowest, of jealousies:
Did'st thou not pay her open compliment
Before thou went'st away, and so give cause
For all to couple thy own name with hers?

ALANCIA.

Elena, yes, thy words are true; but then
I never loved, or thought to marry, her.

ELEANOR.

But was that well in thee, say, Manuel?

ALANCIA.

She has a heart no bigger than her lip.

ELEANOR.

That is too large for one to trifle with.

ALANCIA.

Thou art an angel; yes, thou art, Elena:
But all the court expected it of me.
Remember, I had not seen thee, Elena.

ELEANOR.

And are the expectations of a court
More to Alancia than the demands
Of his own heart and conscience?

ALANCIA (*looking down gravely*).

Of a court?

[*He looks up.*

Thou art a goddess! Until now, Elena,
I knew not women had such thoughts as these.

[*He muses awhile.*

I had revulsions in my soul at times,
When I was sick of all the jealousies;
The selfish plots of one against another;
The sharp provision 'mong the dowagers,
To grasp the fairest portion for their daughters
Who're duping them, meanwhile, at every step;
But in your England, I did surely think
They let the maidens marry whom they loved.

ELEANOR (*sighing*).

No: 'mong the rich and noble 'tis the same.

ALANCIA.

They say it was not so of old in Spain.
Before we learned to ape the ways of France,
We knew of such a thing as truth, — as love:
They know it still in Andalusia.
'Tis held a glory there to live and love,
And fickleness is scorned of high and low;
Their hearts are deep, as are their azure skies;
And, in the mellow twilight, lovers talk
In whispers through the airy lattice gates:
Could we go there, how sweet 'twould be, Elena!

ELEANOR.

O Manuel! I cannot hear such dreams.

ALANCIA.

There I could write, Elena; ay, could write,
With pen of charmēd gold, that should ring out
Such changes on my page, that men should pause
And listen, even as they turn to hear
The bell of the cathedral sounding deep.

ELEANOR.

O Manuel, Manuel! I believe in thee:
That thought shall comfort me, if we must part.

ALANCIA.

We will not part, we will not part; ay, never!

ELEANOR.

Alancia, dost thou not know they wish
To have me wedded to another man?

ALANCIA.

Who is it? Speak his name, for love of heaven.

ELEANOR (*trembling*).

The Señor Everard, my uncle's friend.

ALANCIA.

Ah! 'tis the man who called thee from my side,
With some express or feigned command, one night, —
That summoned thee to Lady Iverton.
That stiff-necked Englishman, who hath not got
Enough of soul to see thy loveliness, —
Pardon, — thy countryman, — I do forget;
I know not good or ill of him: perchance
Thou canst speak better in his favor, say?
No, no: thou dost not love him, my Elena?

ELEANOR.

It will be harder, then, to marry him.

ALANCIA.

Thou shalt not marry him, thou little one.

ELEANOR.

Art thou my keeper, then, best Manuel?
Thou art, indeed, the keeper of my heart;
My uncle waits for my obedience.

ALANCIA.

He shall not, — shall not! Go with me, sweet child,
Unto Gibraltar's English priest, and there
I'll be thy husband: none shall step between.

ELEANOR (*starting back*).

No, Manuel, never. If thou speakest so,
I must not ever, — ever see thee more.

ALANCIA.

Forgive; I'll never think the thought again.
But must I calmly lose thee now, my heaven,
My sweet Elena? God! it shall not be.

ALANCIA.

Be calm, be calm; I'll see thee yet again.

[*Here begins the closing scene of "La Favorita." The monks are heard solemnly chanting in the distance. "La Favorita" comes in, and falls before the cross.* ELENA *and* ALANCIA *turn and look. The house is breathless with attention.*

ALANCIA (*whispering*).

Ah! better see thee so, — given up to heaven, —
Than in the arms of some poor lord of earth,
Who cannot love thee as I love, Elena.

ELEANOR.

I am not shut away from out thy sight.

[*They sit behind the curtain of the box. He holds her hand in his. They look again: the dying lover staggers in.*

And thou, — thou art not dead. Thou art not dead, —
Thy Eleanor can hear thy breathing still,
And feel thy hand so warm, that holds her own:
Thy Eleanor is not all wretched yet.

[ALANCIA *sits pale and silent, holding tightly her hand. The lovers meet in the convent.*

'Tis sweet to doubt, and then believe, like this.
No, no: too late they meet, — too late they meet!
But ah! to die, my Manuel, on thy breast;
To die, e'en now, and end at once with thee
This weariness, this sinking of my soul, —
Thy spirit travelling with me on the way
Unto the blessed land, where I could walk
Through all the sacred hours with thee, my friend,
And none molest: the angels would but smile,
To see us two so happy in their heaven.

[*The curtain falls. The señora in the box arouses from her slumber.*

ALANCIA (*springs up; seizing her hand*).

Dost thou believe in me? Is thy heart mine
For ever, whatsoe'er may be our fate?

ELEANOR.

Yes, I believe, — yes, I am thine till death.

[*He darts out. The Opera closes.*

SCENE II.

Midnight. A street of Madrid. A knot of SPANIARDS *in close conversation.*

THE DUKE OF ALANCIA.

Is it all ready? What is the plan?

FIRST SPANIARD.

First, to make the queen sign the old constitution, at midnight.

ALANCIA.

You cannot force her to do that.

SECOND SPANIARD.

We mean to fetch out one of her lovers, and have a bullet ready to put through his head. That will bring her round, as it did Christina half-a-dozen years ago.

OTHER SPANIARDS (*cheering softly*).

Bravo! bravissimo!

ALANCIA.

What next?

SECOND SPANIARD.

Set on the populace in the morning, with the cry, "Viva la Constitution!" Draw up a line of dragoons opposite the Casa de Positas.

ALANCIA.

Will the Ministry give in, do you think?

SECOND SPANIARD.

Not at first: they will lean on that old bear, Garcia, with his infantry; but we can get him under.

ALANCIA.

Are you so sure of that?

THIRD SPANIARD.

We've got arms and men enough.

THIRD SPANIARD.

Combustible old Figueras will go off like a rocket.

SECOND SPANIARD.

Secretaries of War cannot do much at this late hour.

THIRD SPANIARD.

What a passion the general will be in.

ALANCIA.

I'm not so sure General Figueras hasn't been doing something more than getting into a passion.

FIRST SPANIARD.

I suppose he *is* enlarging the army all he can; but, if we succeed at this crisis, we shall gain a prestige to start with, that will soon demoralize the Government forces.

[*They all separate.*

ALANCIA (*goes away, talking to himself*).

I do not like the way matters are going.

SCENE III.

English Embassy. SIR HENRY *in his office.* *A knock at the door.*

SIR HENRY.

Come in.

[*Enter* ELEANOR, *pale and quiet.*

ELEANOR.

My uncle, I would speak to you,
If I do not intrude upon your time.

SIR HENRY.

No, no: sit down, I'm always glad to see you.

[*She goes up to his table, and stands there.*

ELEANOR (*clearing her voice*).

Some weeks ago, you spoke of Everard:
I only said to you, sir, at the time,
My heart could never yield to your request;
I had not given it then to any man,
But, sir, since then, — I deem it right to tell you, —

I deem it right to keep no truth from you, —
The duke, Don Manuel de Alancia,
Has won my heart unalterably, sir.
I love Don Manuel de Alancia,

[*Blushing deeply.*

And I have told him so; but that you, sir,
Will never look with favor on his suit.

SIR HENRY.

I am indebted to you in this matter,
For taking into view my wishes.

ELEANOR.

Uncle!

SIR HENRY.

Well, well, you have done very right; I'm glad
That you are not deceiving me, my child.

ELEANOR.

'Tis true, indeed, I listened to his love,
And have indulged in very dangerous dreams;
But I did never lead him on to think
That they could end in a reality.

SIR HENRY.

Eleanor, I can never sanction it, —
Your marriage with this Spanish gentleman.

I have no wish to wound your feelings, — no:
But I in conscience cannot give consent;
I have no faith in him, nor in his race, —
No faith in this young aristocracy.

ELEANOR.

You do not know Alancia, my uncle.

SIR HENRY.

I know he is a favorite of the queen;
I know he dabbles all the day in verse,
And compliments the giddy women here.
  You're mad, beside yourself! Good God! my child,
If you so lightly give your confidence,
If you will throw away your happiness,
My arm must stay you at the outset, then.

ELEANOR.

I hear you, sir, and only ask that I
May not be urged to marry Everard.
  Forgive me, uncle, this is all I ask:
It may seem much to you, but not to me,
Who am renouncing, at your will, the best,
The holiest, thing that life has offered me.

SIR HENRY (*coughing a little*).

I did not think you were undutiful;
But that you should delude yourself, — 'tis strange.
What's in this young sprig of nobility?

ELEANOR (*flushing*).

Dear uncle, name him not; it is enough:
You do not hold Alancia in respect:
And we — must part, — you say.

[*Her voice trembles.*

But Everard?

SIR HENRY.

And there you spurn a manly heart as e'er
Was offered to a girl, for this poor duke.

ELEANOR (*her eyes flashing*).

Uncle, insult not, pray, the man I love.

SIR HENRY.

Be it so, then; but you must drive away
Your passion for this Spaniard, and, meanwhile,
I'll speak no more to you of Everard.

[ELEANOR *moves toward the door.*

Stay: I will write, and tell him of my wish.

ELEANOR.

Sir, by your leave, I'll speak to him myself,
And tell him that you say we meet no more;
And — bid farewell to him, if you'll permit.

SIR HENRY.

Whichever way you please: I shall rely
Upon your truth. Appoint an hour to meet

Here in my house, and let the time be brief;
And, after this, I must request that you
Exchange no further words with him. Good-night.

[*Exit* ELEANOR.

SCENE IV.

In SIR HENRY'S *drawing-room a day after. Evening.* ELEANOR *alone. The window is open. She watches a dark figure approaching, wrapt in a cloak, with a sombrero.* ALANCIA *enters the house, ascends to the parlor; enters, seizes her hand, kisses it, and takes a stool at her feet.*

ALANCIA.

Tremble not so; 'tis I, my sweet Elena, —
Thy true Alancia. Look not so pale:
Wilt thou no longer blush with joy to meet
Thy lover? he is but too glad, too gay!

ELEANOR.

My Manuel, we must part, this very night;
And we have but a few short minutes now.
Next week I go unto thy "sunny South,"
Perchance to come here never, never more.

ALANCIA (*springing up fiercely*).

Who dares to say we part?

ELEANOR.

Hush, Manuel!

ALANCIA.

They think to separate us easily;
Ha! Andalusia is not theirs alone.
We'll go to-night, — speak, love; speak, my Elena, —
And they can follow later, when they please.

[*He springs up.*

There is no time to lose; quick, quick, Elena.

ALANCIA.

Alancia, waste no vain words on me,
But comfort thou my heart before I go;
And only tell me that thou lovest me, —
That thou wilt keep me in thy memory
A little when I'm gone: wilt thou, my friend?

ALANCIA (*covering her hand with kisses*).

The Virgin leave me in the direst hour,
If I do cease to think of thee, my all!

ELEANOR.

I shall remember thee, when I am there
Alone, among the fair and glorious spots
Which thou hast told me of; and I shall say
'Twas here he sat, or there he roved along
The river-side, or dreamed among those towers, —
And fancy thou art with me, if I can.
Ah, no! thou'lt not be there, thou'lt not be there.

[*With broken voice.*

We will not say farewell for ever; speak.
Thou wilt not give up thy Elena yet?

ALANCIA.

Give thee up, angel? I will breathless stand
Through all my life, and never cease to hope
Some far-off hour may bring thee back to me,
So long as thou art not another's love.

ELEANOR.

Thanks, Manuel: he said that he would wait;
My uncle will not ask me yet to wed.
A little time, my love, I still shall have,
A little time to keep thee in my heart,
Ere 'twill be wrong to think thy very name.

[*She hears her uncle's impatient step.*

O Manuel, he comes! Farewell, farewell.

[*He springs towards her. She throws herself upon his breast.*

ALANCIA.

Promise that thou wilt keep thyself for me,
Till heaven may be more kind to us again.

[*He kisses her passionately.*

Thou shalt be mine, thou shalt be mine, Elena!
I'll follow thee: no one shall dare forbid.

ELEANOR.

I cannot speak to thee, Alancia.

ALANCIA.

But I can see thee, — see thee, little one.

ELEANOR (*hearing footsteps*).

Haste, haste; he thinks that thou hast gone away.
He'll summon me. Farewell, Alancia.

ALANCIA.

Adios, my Elena: God preserve thee.
Remember, we shall meet, — shall meet again.

[*He tears himself away.* ELEANOR *goes to her apartment.*

SCENE V.

In the house of the DUCHESS OF ALANCIA. DOÑA MARIA *and the duke. The duke is walking up and down his apartment at night. The moon shines into his room. His mother enters softly.*

DOÑA MARIA.

Ah Manuel! thy poor mother cannot sleep
While thou art pacing all the weary night.

[*She takes his hand. They sit down by the window.*

Son of my soul, may I not stay with thee?

[*Tears come into his eyes, which he brushes quickly away.*

ALANCIA.

All things go wrong with me, I think, my mother.

DOÑA MARIA.

Dost thou so love the English girl, my son?
I know she must be beautiful and good,
Else would no brave and manly heart like thine
Lose all its joy and lightsomeness for her.

ALANCIA (*kissing her hand*).

Thanks, thanks, sweet mother: now thou speakest well,
Thou givest me a little happiness.

DOÑA MARIA.

And can it be she does not love thee, son, —
My handsome, gallant Manuel, who art
The very picture of thy father now?
If thou dost woo as well as he did me,
How can she turn a cold cheek to thee, son?

ALANCIA.

Mother, she loves me, — like an angel, too.

DOÑA MARIA.

Then wherefore this despondency, my son?

ALANCIA.

Her uncle has forbidden us to meet:
I fear that she must wed another man.

DOÑA MARIA.

Ah! then I have no heart to chide thee, son.
I did reproach thee harshly at the first;
I thought it was the passion of a boy;
But now I'll weep with thee. Thy mother's tears
Are all thine own: naught hath she now to do,
But to be sad and grieving for thy sake.

Dost thou remember, son, how many days
We've idly sat, and laughed away the hours,
When I was mother, sister, comrade, too,
And oft drew smiles at my lost dignity?
Thy father, clouded with the smoke of wars,
Would gaze with eyes of pleasure on us both,
And rest his wearied looks upon our sport;
And call us to his knee, his two delights, —
His Maria and his brave Manuel;
And when Our Lady took him, Manuel,

[*She sobs.*

We two grew old together then; but ah!
Thy mother fastest, for a sudden pang
Went through her soul, thou could'st not haply know.
But now thou art her all, and she will do
Whate'er thou'lt ask, to make thee smile again.
Cheer up thy soul; I'll go with thee, my son,
To all the lovely lands that thou canst name.
We'll sit together 'neath the whispering trees,
Or by the ruins thou dost love so much,
And thou shalt have thy paper and thy pen;
Nor will I frown, but joy to see thee write.

ALANCIA.

Mother, no more, I pray, of foreign lands;
I'm sick of them, of all their petty sights
And flat varieties. Ambition, too,
I hate it; I will go and dig the earth,

And eat and sleep, before I'll touch again
A mawkish pen; descanting, in sweet words,
Of things which other happy men possess,
While I am paling o'er a sheet of paper.

DOÑA MARIA.

But is thy mother nothing, then, to thee?
Because that thou hast loved another more,
Hast thou no single thought for her, my son?

ALANCIA.

Dear mother, pardon, pardon: I am hard
And evil in my heart; rebellion cold
Is working in my breast, and freezing all
The good in me to selfish, dark defiance.
If God would give me but the joy I ask,
My heart would never have less room for thee
Because Elena lived in it besides.

DOÑA MARIA.

Ah! well, I'll not be jealous, child; no, no:

[*She rises to go.*

But go thou to thy bed, and rest awhile.
Forget not now the Virgin's love and pity;
Pray, in her name, for peace and consolation.
Promise, my son, thou wilt not tear thy soul;
Rest thee on Jesus' breast; all may be well.

[*She moves out. He springs up, follows her, and embraces her fondly, neither speaking. She goes out, and he retires.*

SCENE VI.

Two SPANIARDS *in a lonely street, at night.*

FIRST SPANIARD.

The thing is ripe for bursting. God be with us!

SECOND SPANIARD.

Not ripe; but it may burst at any hour.
We cannot hold together long, I think.

FIRST SPANIARD.

O for an hour of Espartero, Parco!

SECOND SPANIARD.

Why does he stay there on that little farm?

FIRST SPANIARD.

Was he not bound in honor to be silent?

SECOND SPANIARD.

Yes, to Narvaez: but the times have changed.

FIRST SPANIARD.

He was an honest patriot, and a brave.

SECOND SPANIARD.

Yes, I believe him incorruptible.

FIRST SPANIARD.

Some think he was too dainty with the Carlists.

SECOND SPANIARD.

It was the only prudent course to take.

FIRST SPANIARD.

And if Christina had not marred his plans,
We should be free enough, this hour, in Spain.

SECOND SPANIARD.

A little of his prudence now in us
Would give me greater hope that we should win.
What's that?

[*He starts.*

FIRST SPANIARD.

You are not growing nervous, Parco?

[*A watchman is heard.*

WATCHMAN.

Ave Maria! Pu - - - ris - - - sima - - -
A las once han da - - - do - - - y se - - - re - - - no.

SECOND SPANIARD.

Yes, I confess, at every sound I hear,
I think the populace is rising up:
If we were only well prepared for it!

FIRST SPANIARD.

Well, we must trust in God, and do our best.
Yonder seréno says that all is well;
We'll take his word for it, and go to rest.

[*Exeunt.*

SCENE VII.

Calle Mayor. Madrid. A body of soldiers advancing, cavalry behind them, the populace crying " Viva la Constitution." GARCIA, head of the royal forces, in general's uniform, mounted on his horse, dashes at full gallop in among the crowd, with a drawn sword in his hand, followed by two officers only and a few dragoons. A panic spreads among the crowd; the soldiers waver; bullets are flying in every direction. GARCIA spurs his horse in and out of the crowd, crying " Long live the Queen." The rabble retires by the Alcala. A bullet grazes his hat. He rides down the men, and demands of the cavalry officer his surrender. The officer yields up his sword. The revolutionists are defeated.

SCENE VIII.

In a Café.

FIRST SPANIARD.

So the liberals are done up.

SECOND SPANIARD.

The thing wasn't ripe; they suspected treason, and had to precipitate matters.

FIRST SPANIARD.

That old devil, Garcia, did the work handsomely.

SECOND SPANIARD.

It was mere force of will that accomplished it. He had no power actually, but he made the men think he had.

FIRST SPANIARD.

There's the thing; there he proves that he is a great general: it took no little courage to do what he did.

SECOND SPANIARD.

Tut! here comes a lot of them.

[*A party of Government soldiers enter, and seat themselves around a bowl of chocolate, singing,* —

Ta ra ra ra,
Pro - gre - sis - ta,
There you are, — you are.

SCENE IX.

The Duke of Alancia *pacing up and down the room, holding a letter in his hand.*

Why did I ever mix my hand in this, —
This muddy sea of Spanish politics,
To be so cursed with such an offer now?
Ah! I was sick of being a poet: yes,
Yes, that was it. *She* loved me for it, though,

And that was sweet. 'Tis sweet indeed; but yet
I only sang into the ears of men,
And they were pleased awhile, and turned away.
The old man sneered: I longed to act, — to act,
And do some deeds which e'en an Englishman
Could see with eyes of flesh, and comprehend.

[*He muses awhile.*

God knows the fate of my compatriots!
But me they think to buy with liberty;
To let me off if I will serve their ends, —
These miserable agents of the crown.
Why did I ever bow and dance among
The ladies of the court, until my queen
Looked on and smiled, and called me to her side,
But to insult me deeply in the end?
It was not she: those loyal statesmen there,
Have told her she can flatter me to do
A traitor act, in payment for her smiles;
They think to recommend their policy,
And make it decent in the people's eyes,
By my dead father's honorable name,
Who never drew his sword for tyranny,
And scorns me from the skies, if I do yield
Unto the coward thought of stepping so
Upon the Spanish people's liberty, —
My note will show them I am not so base.
I'm lost! I'm lost! save in the eyes of heaven,
For I lose *her*. The cause by which I hoped
To gain a new respect in my own eyes,

And earn her fairly by the strike for freedom,
Has ruined me, — it drives me from her face.

Yes, I must go: I could not be their tool,
Ev'n though it set me in the chair of gods.
I know they will inflame the kindly queen,
And drive me on to instant banishment. —
Thou art not ruined; no, Alancia:
Dost thou not carry thy soul firm and true?
And in that other land to which we tend,
Beyond the feverish turmoil of this earth,
She'll smile and say, "I knew thou wast not base."

[*A servant enters with a note, and retires.*

ALANCIA (*turning pale*).

What! is't so soon? I had not thought they dared
To hunt me from my home so quick.

[*He opens and reads.*

To the most excellent Señor Don Manuel, Duke of Alancia.

You are hereby commanded to quit Spain in the space of one hour, in obedience to the order of Her August Majesty, the Queen Isabella II.

Good God, the fawning hounds are on me, then!
My note was courteous, but ah! it cut
Their sorest spots; and now they chase me down.

But I am right: I have the right, — the right.
Farewell, Elena, I must go from thee.

Dear one, if I believed thou wouldst not grieve,
'Twould be a little drop of peace to me.
God! I'll not weep. I will be firm, and go.

[*Exit.*

SCENE X.

The next day. English Embassy. ELEANOR *is sitting alone at home, watching intently the passers-by in the streets. She at length turns, and sighs heavily. A rustling is heard at the door. A* LADY, *dressed in black, with a mantilla drawn close about her face, enters quickly.*

LADY.

A thousand pardons for this liberty.
It is, I think, the Señorita Manton.

ELEANOR (*rising*).

It is, señora: seat yourself, I pray.

[*She throws up her veil.*

LADY.

O señorita! tell me, — tell me quick,
Where is my son? where is the duke, my son?
Before you is his mother: yes, you see
Doña Maria de Alancia;
If you know where he is, I pray you tell.
I come not now to sue or to reproach;
A mother only seeks her missing son.

ELEANOR (*turning pale*).

Señora, I know not; is he not here?
I saw him three nights since, and he was well.

DOÑA MARIA (*scanning her*).

You speak the truth; I see it in your face.
[*Wringing her hands.*
You cannot help a widowed mother, then.

They say that he is gone away from Spain:
But I will not believe such idle tales, —
That he was seen on horseback, riding through
The city gates that lead unto Granada;
And that his passports certify he goes
To Malaga, and sails for Italy.
O Italy! 'tis far, 'tis far away.

[ELEANOR *looks at her bewildered, and then falls speechless to the floor.*

Ah, niña mia! did'st thou love him so?

[*She stoops to lift her up, and bathes her temples with water from the table.*

Then 'twas not thou who sent him from his home?
Rash boy, to give himself up to despair,
When this sweet creature lives, and loves him so!
How wilful, how perverse he is! how strange,
To throw up madly every chance of hope!

[ELEANOR, *meanwhile, opens her eyes.*

I was most jealous of thee until now:
I kept the passion down, but oh! how burned

My hatred unto thee, when first I thought
He'd taken leave of thee, and me forgot:
But now thou art in grief as well as me,
And more, — I know of something else beside
A mother's love, for I have been a wife.

[ELEANOR *seizes her hand, kisses it, while the tears run down.*

Ah! wheresoe'er he is, ungrateful son,
I've found a daughter now, in losing him.

ELEANOR (*starting*).

You have not lost him; think not so, señora.

DOÑA MARIA.

'Tis a far country, there, beyond the sea:
Yes, let him leave his widowed mother, then,

[*Her eyes flash.*

We two will shake him off our injured hearts.

[*She strikes her breast.* ELEANOR *looks up frightened.*

No, no: my Manuel, what evil eye
Hath cast its falsest glances over thee?

[*She bursts into tears, and crosses herself.*

He's gone, he's gone: could'st thou not keep him, lady?
Long since his mother gave up all her power,
But thou, — could'st thou not hold him by thy side,
In grief as well as joy, suspense as hope?

[ELEANOR *looks at her beseechingly.*

Pardon me, little daughter, —

[*She embraces her.*

Ah! 'tis strange, —
Most strange.

But he was never faithless yet:
My Manuel was strange, but never false.

ELEANOR.

I do believe your son is true, señora.

DOÑA MARIA.

Yes, thou art right, he's true in heart: but then —
Perchance, it is a wayward freak; perchance
He will come back and make us happy yet.

ELEANOR (*looking fixedly at her*).

I know not now the end of this, señora;
But, if I was the cause of pain to you,
Believe it has not been without the cost
To me of all my peace and happiness, —
No single heart to share my confidence.

DOÑA MARIA.

Thou hast this heart, — Doña Maria's heart:
Yes, thou hast gained me quite, thou young Inglesa.
I do not wonder that he wept for thee.

ELEANOR (*she falls on* DOÑA MARIA'S *neck*).

I thank you: God reward your heart, señora.

DOÑA MARIA (*she rises at length, and walks up and down the room*).

What offering shall I make unto the Church
Of San Francisco, — to his patron saint?

I make a vow, — I'll wear no gown but this,
Nor visit any earthly place, except
The altar of the blessed Virgin there,
Until I see my son, alive or dead.

ELEANOR.

Señora, where is Don Fermin Morales?
Maybe he'll have some brighter news to tell.

DOÑA MARIA.

I'll go and see what more they say of him.
Adios, daughter; may the saints protect thee!

[*She embraces her, weeping, and hurries out.*

ELEANOR (*alone. She covers her face with her hands, and the tears trickle through*).

Can it be possible he gives me up?
'Tis true we cannot speak; but why, — but why
In such a haste to take himself away?
He who was begging me to leave my home, —
Could he not wait a little while for me?
Must run into another land, and leave
Me here to breast my troubles all alone?

[*She sobs convulsively.*

I am alone, — alone. Ah! she is kind,
But she has not a word to say for him:
She thinks that he — I saw it in her face —
Is wearied, vexed, with his unlucky love.
She blames him, too; but I, — I should not *blame:*

He's wearied with it all, is he? Good God!
There is no more of him, if that is true;
There is no Manuel de Alancia
Like him, I knew; nor ever was there one:
He is nowhere on earth, nor in the heavens.

[*She weeps aloud, then rises and hurries towards the door. She stops. Pulls a little cord on her neck.*

This cross is cold as ice upon my breast:
It feels as though his hand were resting there, —
So strange and chill; but they were warm, I think, —
His fingers, — when he placed it on my neck.
Why should I keep it now?

[*She takes it off.*

But no, I cannot:
I'll wear it for Christ's sake, if not for his.

[*She puts it on again, and goes to her room.*

PART V.

SCENE I.

Some weeks have passed. On the road to Sevilla, before daybreak. The driver of the diligence is singing,—

Anda! Anda! the mountains are clear;
Anda! Anda! the morning is sweet:
The clouds are all bright'ning, the swift sun is near,
O mule of my soul, be light with thy feet!
My girl will come out to meet us with the day;
Up, up, Coronel, up, up, and away.
A talk we will keep,
While the passengers sleep:
Thou only canst tell
What we say, Coronel.

[*A head appears at the diligence window interrupting him.*

LADY IVERTON.

Ho, mayoral! when shall we reach Sevilla?

MAYORAL.

A half-a-dozen leagues or more, señora.

LADY IVERTON.

You promised we should be there at the dawn.

MAYORAL.

Ay, ay, señora; but the roads are bad:
The poor beasts cannot go a league a minute.
[*To the boy goading the mules.*
S - - st! Jose, boy; you've broken sticks enough.

BOY.

Ea, ea! I've used up all the brush there is,
On Pardo's tenderest side: I'll give it up.
Go on, señor, and God be with you. Ha!
[*Boy turns backward.*

MAYORAL (*alone*).

These foreign folk are always in a hurry;
San Pedro! but what business have their worships
To be awake at cock-crowing? La-la-la - - -

That little señorita speaks as sweet
As any Española in the world.
The old one, — foh! when she came off her seat
So grand, one day, and tumbled in my arms,
It took the stiff'ning out of her a bit.
Fa-la-la, - - - fa-la-la-la.

JUANA (*inside*).

Señora, he will rouse the señorita.

MAYORAL (*he appears at the diligence window with his bread and oranges. He offers them to* LADY IVERTON).

Señora, will you have some of my breakfast?

LADY IVERTON.

Excuse me.

(*Aside.*)

What impertinence, — the peasant!

ELEANOR (*leaning forward*).

I'll take some with you: thank you, mayoral.

MAYORAL.

Ah, señorita! you are then awake;
I fear it is not good enough for you.

[*He hands her the oranges, and a long roll of white bread. She takes some.*

That Madrilena there will sleep till noon.

[*Turning towards* JUANA.

JUANA.

Your pardon, hombre, I was not asleep:
I marvel who could rest with all your clatter.
And I'm no Madrilena either, thank you.

MAYORAL.

Where may it be yóu come from, then, my daughter?

JUANA.

Estremadura, may it please your worship.

MAYORAL.

Ah ha! they brought you up on cheese-curds there?

JUANA.

I lived as well as you do, any day, —
Who buy your yard of bread when you are hungry,
And poke it down your throat with ends of garlic.

MAYORAL.

Soft, soft! I'm sorry that I spoiled her nap.

[*He goes up on his box, singing.*

I want no nap, nap, nap,
When the sun goes tap, tap, tap,
On my window pane,
Away o'er the plain,
Away with the merry muleteer.

Jingle softly, jingle sweet,
Jingle little bells complete,
Down my buskins to my feet.

ELEANOR (*dropping the oranges and bread in her lap*).

The morning that I longed so for is come,
And now the night seems sweeter. I must look,
When we come near Sevilla; for he said
She glistened like a jewel 'mong her groves.

[*She sighs, and looks at her watch.*

How swift the light is coming in the east.

[*The others fall asleep again. She looks out.*

Oh, what a lonely Moorish tower that is!
These sights of old were never gloomy to me.

[*She closes her eyes and sits silent.*

SCENE II.

Sevilla. ELEANOR *is sitting by a window, overlooking a court, leaning her head upon her hand.*

JUANA.

Poor señorita, you are weary still!
The diligence is rumbling in your head,
I do believe. Carámba! How I longed
To start the mules off in a lively trot!
The night we found ourselves so fast in mud,
You laughed: it was the first time on the way;
The fat Valencian prayed, though, in the corner;
While I, betwixt you, started for the door.
My soul! Who wants to be ground up beneath
A dozen trunks, and mayoral on top?

ELEANOR.

Juana, I've had time enough to rest.
[*She rouses up as Juana looks at her.*
How soft and fragrant is the air, Juana!
I would not stir, but sit here all the day:
'Tis gentler than Granada, is it not?

JUANA.

Ay, señorita: precious little good
The air is doing you. No, no: you had
More roses once upon your cheek than now;

They used to start and brighten up of old,
When you came in so lovely from your walks.
But now you never change, — 'tis all the same;
Or, if you smile, it seems to come so hard,
I would as lief see tears: ah, madre mia!

[*She hums a tune.*

Vamos! my little señorita; vamos!
I'll bring your fan to you, and your mantilla;
You will be gayer for a morning walk;
The streets, — they are so gay! Hark! now I hear
The guitars all a-tinkling round the corners:
Hola! Upon my faith, 'tis the Bolero
They're dancing now! Look, señorita, look!

[*She runs nearer the window. An old woman and a young man are dancing.*

Ha! ha! that neat muchacho might have got
A girl a trifle younger, I do think.

[*She shakes with laughter.*

Ha! ha! She turns her toes out very well;
They must be old and stiff; if twenty years
Were taken off of her, I'd say it was
As fair a piece of dancing as I'd wish.

[*She sings while she watches them.*

Ay, ay! I confess, good padre,
Though I love sweet Cristo's madre,
And the rows of saints so blessed, —
Padre, thou hast rightly guesséd.
I do love to trip it, skip it,
With a handsome Andaluz;

If he looketh young and well,
I forget the chapel bell;
If he looks from out one eye,
On to prayers, — let him go by!
Ay, ay, ay.

Ah, madre mia! I'd not grieve me much
If I should never see Madrid again.

ELEANOR (*looking up*).

What's that you said of Madrid, then, Juana?

[JUANA *does not hear, but still watches the dancers.*

ELEANOR (*musing*).

No: I regret not that I told him so.
Can I deny the truth of what she says?
What *do* I gain in payment for the grief
And disappointment I inflict on him,
My good old uncle? He is sad, she says,
And weighed with care and trouble. Is it so?
What is there left for me? What joy have I
That I should treasure up my heart, and hold
So dear my precious self? What wait I for?

[*She thinks awhile.*

I'll marry him; he's been most kind of late:
'Twill give some pleasure unto those I love,
To whom I am indebted much; and I, —
I think I shall have no more now to suffer.
They're gone together, — both my grief and joy:
What matters it whose name I'm called by now?

But ah! to be a wife, a new-made wife,
With nothing of the pride that dignifies
The strange unwonted part; no lovely joy
To drive away all anxious perturbation!

[*She muses again.*

Three months it is since first we left Madrid, —
Since he, Alancia, passed the city gates.
Did he, perchance, remorsefully look back,
As through his soul the thought of me might flash?
Or did he drown his vexing memories
Amid the clatter of his horse's step,
Till, reaching once the shores of Italy,
Amid the glowing charmers all around,
My image would no more disturb his peace?

[*She springs up.*

No, no: away! I thought I'd done with this.

'*Tis* lovely here, Juana; thou art right:
I'll go and walk with thee. Be ready, — quick!

[*Exeunt* ELEANOR *and* JUANA.

SCENE III.

A week later. SIR HENRY AND LADY IVERTON.

LADY IVERTON.

You say she came to you a week ago,
Consenting to it of her own accord.

SIR HENRY.

Yes, yes. You do not think she takes the thing
So hard of late?

LADY IVERTON.

Why, no: you see she does not.
You said, yourself, you had not urged the matter;
She's given Alancia up; she seems, in fact,
Chagrined about this silly freak of love.

SIR HENRY.

So, then, you think she's thrown the matter off,
And grows more like herself since we came here.

LADY IVERTON.

Of course I do. She treats poor Everard
With much less *brusquerie*, I mark, of late;
And she is far more gracious to us all.
Believe me, 'twill come out well in the end.
You fixed on this next Friday, did you not,
To have the wedding? There's no time to lose.
Dear me; I must arrange about the cards.

[*She turns to go out.*

SIR HENRY.

You say they're gone to the cathedral.

LADY IVERTON.

Yes.

SIR HENRY.

I do not like to have her hover round
These gloomy places: no, it does not suit me.
If she's in spirits, why does she not dress,
And go along the pleasant river banks,
And see the people moving on the walks.

LADY IVERTON.

La, Iverton, you talk so like a man!
'Tis not the fashion to go there so early.

SIR HENRY.

The devil take the fashion. I suppose
The sun's no more in vogue than in Madrid,
Where they roll out so lazily at night,
And trundle in their sleepy carriages.

LADY IVERTON.

Never you fear; she always had a taste
For groping round in lonely spots, you know:
She went to all the churches in Madrid.

SIR HENRY.

Well, well; perhaps you're right: I think 'tis so;
But yet, — I never called her melancholy.

LADY IVERTON.

No; 'tis her way: you cannot change her nature.

SIR HENRY.

Heigh-ho! 'tis hard to suit these girls at best,
Such different stuff you women are from us.

LADY IVERTON.

Well, well; her pride is mortified, of course:
She will not throw off her chagrin at once.

SIR HENRY (*musing*).

At all events, I'm doing what is best:
In two months she may thank me for my pains.

LADY IVERTON.

We take the boat to-morrow for Gibraltar?

SIR HENRY.

Yes, yes; I gave you all directions once.

LADY IVERTON.

The consul and the English bishop there,
You've not forgotten them? About the cards —

SIR HENRY.

Do what you please: consult with Eleanor.

[*Exeunt.*

SCENE IV.

ELEANOR *and* JUANA *walking in the streets of Seville.*

ELEANOR (*to herself*).

There is a song, — 'tis running in my mind: —

" Adieu, thou wert most fond and false.
. . . Why should I waste my very soul on thee?"

Doth fondness ever go with fickleness?

[*She turns toward the cathedral.*

JUANA.

What, señorita! will you go to church?
You're good enough: you have no need to pray;
A livelier place to-day will suit you better.

ELEANOR.

My poor Juana! I do wish thou had'st
A gayer mistress. But we'll see the shops
When we come back; and I will buy for thee
A pair of pretty gilded pins, like those
The Andaluzas wear within their veils.

JUANA.

Mil gracias, Señorita Eleanor!

[*They enter the cathedral. An old woman holds out her hand at the door.*

Señora, pity, for the love of God!

JUANA (*pushing her off*).

Silence thee, woman; let the lady be!

ELEANOR (*hands her money; she goes off blessing her*).

The love of God! ah, that I would not lose!
The earth is cruel; heaven may be more kind.

[*She walks up the aisle. The organ is reverberating loud and full. She sits down on a stone step.*

Ah, how divine it is! It stills my heart.

[*She sits listening.*

I am not thinking of my sins enough,
It may be. Yes, perhaps I've loved too well.
No, no, my Master, I forgot thee never;
In thy name prayed I, every step I went,
To be delivered from temptation. Hark!
How roll the trembling sounds majestical!
What is this grief of mine? It sinks away
Before this great Infinity of love,
Around us pressing, calm, intense, and full,
But answering ever unto mortals seeking.

[*She sits silent awhile, and then rises up.*

I have a longing once again to see
The old monk of Ribera hanging there
Within that little, solemn, lonely chapel:
I'll try to find the spot.

[*She looks into the side chapels as she passes.*

Ah, what a world of beautiful retreats!
Within this mighty space I'll lose myself,
Nor e'er be found again, perchance.

'Tis strange;
I cast a glance upon the saint one day,
Alone there in the dim and mellow light,
Nor thought of him again; till now he comes,
So calm, distinct, so loftily before me,
I must go further, till I see his face.

[*She passes here and there a solitary kneeler.*

If I could stay for ever here, nor go
Again into the sick'ning, lightsome streets.

[*She finds the chapel at length, and goes in. She stands gazing at the picture.*

He too has suffered, and maybe with love
As well as martyrdom for holy faith;
And yet there's joy upon his lifted brow:
I am not good enough to rise beyond
The pains of earth.

[*The tears run slowly down her cheek. She turns to go out. A dark, muffled figure passes by the chapel, without looking up. She trembles, and leans against a pillar inside; then draws a long breath.*

My foolish heart! but 'twas so like *his* step:

[*The figure turns, passes again, and casts a hasty glance, and goes on.*

He wore his cloak just so about his face.

[*The figure turns again, passes, and scans her intently. She trembles.*

How can another Spaniard look like him!

[*He comes back again, looks fixedly, vacillates, turns, looks again, then throws down his cloak, and springs forward.*

Elena, is it thou? Speak, — speak to me!

ELEANOR (*gasping out*).

Alancia, Alancia!

[*She holds her hand to her heart, totters, and falls*

ALANCIA (*he stoops to raise her*).

Elena, look! it is thy Manuel.

ELEANOR (*opening her eyes at length confusedly*).

My Manuel, — he went away long since:
Forgive me, uncle; I was dreaming, then,
That he came back; but 'tis all over now.

ALANCIA.

Elena, '*tis* thy lover: see, 'tis he!

ELEANOR (*starts up, and looks at him*).

Alancia, how dar'st thou meet me now?

ALANCIA (*drawing a long breath*).

Ah! then 'tis not thy spirit that I see?

ELEANOR (*drawing away*).

What matters it to thee if it be I
Or not, Alancia?

ALANCIA.

I know, — I know

[*She disengages herself.*

Thou dost belong unto another now, —
Thou bear'st his name, — no more my own Elena:

But I have sworn to see thee once again,
Whatever husband dare to step between.

ELEANOR.

What mean you by these words, Alancia?

ALANCIA.

I mean I loved you, lady, ere he claimed
You for his wife. If you so soon forget
What 'tis I mean, yet have not I, indeed.

ELEANOR.

Pardon; I am not wedded to him yet.

ALANCIA.

Not his! not his! Speak, for the love of heaven!

ELEANOR.

Why should you care to know, Don Manuel?

ALANCIA (*with broken voice*).

Elena, time has worked most fast with thee!
Elena, art thou free, and yet so changed?

ELEANOR.

Answer me by your sacred faith, my friend!
Why did you leave me so, Don Manuel?
You knew my grief: why did you leave me so,
Without a parting word, alone, amid
The fears with which my heart was almost breaking?

ALANCIA.

Did'st thou not see the note I sent to thee?

ELEANOR.

No, not a word, — a word, Alancia.

ALANCIA.

Did'st thou not know that I was forced to go?

ELEANOR.

No, no: I thought that thou wast tired of me.

ALANCIA.

Did'st thou not see my answer from thy aunt?

ELEANOR.

No, never. Cruel woman; yes, 'twas she!
And did'st thou write unto thy Eleanor,
And go away with her cold, wicked words?

ALANCIA.

I prayed thee not to wed this Everard;
I told thee I would yet come back to thee.
Love, I was fleeing for my liberty.
She said thou wast betrothēd to this man;
That 'twas thy wish to hear no more from me.
I had no time to lose: I dashed away, —
No hope, except in thy heart's constancy.

ELEANOR (*a tear rolls down her cheek*).

Ah! how could she be so unkind, unkind!

[*She tries to rise, and totters.*

ALANCIA.

Let us go out into the open air.

[*He helps her out of the cathedral.* JUANA *spies them, and runs after them. He sends her to the street for a carriage; it arrives. He turns to* JUANA, *hands her money, which she refuses.*

Go thou upon thy way, my good Juana;
Say not a word of me —

JUANA.

Bien, caballero.

[*He springs in after* ELEANOR, *and they drive to the Buen Retiro, which is quite deserted.*

ELEANOR (*sinking back exhausted*).

If I had known that thou wast true, my heart
Had been most light through all the darkest hours.
What was the fear of other men to this?
This deadly sinking when I thought thee false?

[*He takes her in his arms, strokes her hair, and looks at her without speaking. She lifts up her head suddenly, and looks at him.*

Art thou the same, the very same, as then?

ALANCIA.

I am too happy now, Elena, love,
To take thee much to task for words like these, —

For all thy doubting. I am so content
With seeing thy dear face again to-day,
I will not speak of how I loved and suffered.
  It is enough to be with thee once more:
We will forget our griefs, nor throw away
This hour, the gift of heaven to us, Elena.

[*He draws her head to his breast.*

ELEANOR.

Ah, this is rest, — 'tis rest! I thought my head
Would never lie upon thy breast again.
Would'st thou have liked another head as well?

ALANCIA.

Think'st thou a woman's head should ever rest
Where I have felt the touch of thy soft hair?

ELEANOR (*starting up suddenly*).

Manuel, I have accepted Everard's hand!
To-morrow, we are going to Gibraltar!

ALANCIA

Gibraltar?

ELEANOR.

Yes: thou knowest why.

ALANCIA.

By heaven,

Thou shalt not go!

ELEANOR.

And he will start to-day.

ALANCIA.

The villain! let him wait and see how good
'Tis to be cheated. Yes: we'll tell him, too,
A fairer lie than she did me. We'll send
Him word that thou art wedded to another:
Maybe 'twill turn to truth before he sees us.

ELEANOR (*drawing away*).

No, no: he is not bad; he has a right —

[*She looks at him fixedly.*

My friend, I must go home.

[*Her looks compel him. He gives the order to the coachman. They both sit in silence. Ere long the carriage enters the street.*

ELEANOR (*terrified*).

We're there! we're there!

[*She bursts into a passion of tears, and clings to him.*

I cannot go to him: no; never, never.

ALANCIA.

Stay, then; stay, then. Go with me to Gibraltar!

ELEANOR.

No, no, Alancia. Ask me not that.

[*She springs up, and looks at him earnestly.*

Alancia, I will not go to him.
I'll lose thee for my duty's sake; but him
I will not take into thy place.

ALANCIA (*eagerly*).

Art sure?
Art sure, Elena?

ELEANOR.

Yes, I've said the word—
I've said it, and I will not take it back.
Be sure the porter seeth not thy face.

[*She alights. He discharges the coachman, draws his hat and cloak about his face, and disappears.* ELEANOR *goes in breathless, and faints. The heavy door clangs after her. She meets* EVERARD *coming down the wide iron staircase. She starts.*

EVERARD (*smiling*).

You start; you see I am not off to-day:
I am too stingy of your company
To go before you, and it is as well.
You'll pardon, will you not, my fickleness?

[*She tries to speak.*

Why, Eleanor, how very pale you are!
You've walked too far, beneath this broiling sun.

[*He offers her his arm to assist her up stairs.*

ELEANOR.

I thank you: I am very tired, in truth.

[*Her arm trembles in his. He conducts her in, and to a sofa.*

EVERARD.

Shall I not ring for wine, or some refreshment?

ELEANOR.

No: I'll go to my room, and rest awhile.

[*He looks solicitous.*

I shall be better, thank you, by and by.

[*She leans back exhausted. He raises the window.*

EVERARD.

The air is fresh that blows in from this side.

[*He looks at her, then pours a glass of water, and sets it by her, and goes towards the door. He turns again, irresolute, and places a cushion at her feet, and moves towards the door; then again he looks back.*

Eleanor, you're not ill, — not ill, I hope?

ELEANOR (*rising up with great effort*).

No, no: be not alarmed; I'll go and rest.

[*He opens the door reluctantly, and goes out.* ELEANOR *retires to her own room.*

SCENE V.

The next morning. EVERARD, *in his apartment, sitting and looking out of the window.*

A dismal, rainy day; so we must wait,
Sir Henry says: to-morrow may be fairer.

Well, well, I care not if we wait for ever.
Why am I grown so thin-of-skin, — so like
A love-sick boy, despairing at a frown?
Away with this poor sentimentalism!
I sought a wife: I've found one to my mind.
She'd do me honor in whatever state,
Nor blind my eyes with women's trickeries:
My taste kept pace along with my discretion.
But I loved, too, — by heavens, I have loved *her!*

[*He muses awhile.*

She is not very gay at sight of me,
That's plain; but I must take what I can get.
I swear now I am ready to renounce
My fondest schemes, if she would only love me;
I *have* been true to her; she knows it not.
Yes, I would throw up every thing this hour
For one approving smile upon her face.

[*He sighs.*

I'm but a sorry bridegroom for to-morrow;
Yet, when I meet her, I shall be a cool,
Contented gentleman as e'er was seen.
Confound it, — but I cannot help my nature, —
Why can't I blaze out like these foreigners?

I am a miserable fellow. Yes,
With all my brilliant prospects opening now
Before the eyes of men, I cannot make
A truthful English girl respect or love me.
I have not lied to her in word or deed.

Where is the lie? Is't in my life? If so,
It never shone out plain till I saw her.

Heigh-ho! there's no use moping o'er my case:
I'll go and walk this sober fit away.

[*Exit.*

SCENE VI.

Café in Sevilla. Two hours later. EVERARD *and a friend.*

GENTLEMAN

You've heard the news that's flying round the town?

EVERARD (*leaning back abstractedly*).

No: has the Duchess of Montpensier
Got a new Paris gown? or have the duke
And she fall'n out, for a variety?

GENTLEMAN.

Oh! you are wide beyond the mark, my man:
You'd hit it nearer if you'd said the queen
Had fallen out just now, and with herself.
The duke, Don Manuel de Alancia,
Is back from Italy: he has been seen
About the town, in many different parts.
The story's out, and he's no loser by it;
'Tis going like wildfire all about the streets.

EVERARD.

What story? Umph! the very word's enough
To make a Spaniard prick his ears up straight.

GENTLEMAN.

It seems that he was mixt up with the party
That made the recent move for liberty.
The Ministry resolved to pardon him, —
To tender him some office of distinction,
And win him thus forever to their side.
They knew how much beloved the old duke was,
And thought to carry measures through the son,
Which else would not be swallowed by the people.
They meant to crowd upon their liberties.

EVERARD.

Well, did not he accept?

GENTLEMAN.

No: he declined,
Most firmly and respectfully, the offer;
Saying he could not carry out the views
The advisers of her majesty required,
And answer to his country and his conscience.
The Cabinet was in a rage, of course;
The queen was half inclined to overlook it:
But they must buzz around her majesty,
And represent to her that he had paid
An insult to her throne and government.
So, then, a royal order came forthwith,

Commanding him to quit the Spanish soil, —
Unless he should retract the words he'd said, —
On pain of his imprisonment and death.
He would not yield, but fled to Italy.
The people will be ready in Madrid
To take him on their shoulders now, they say.

EVERARD.

Have you this all from good authority?

GENTLEMAN.

O yes! there is no question of its truth:
To-morrow's papers will be full of it.
I have a friend who's just from Italy:
He saw the duke. He says he has a soul
As fine as ever ripened in the south.
His fame there as a dramatist is wide;
And all the men of literary note
In Rome and Florence sought his company,
Although he kept himself from gayeties.

EVERARD.

Your friend is of a turn enthusiastic.
But how does't happen that he's back again,
If he so bravely faced them, as you say,
And ran off honorably for conscience' sake?

GENTLEMAN.

Wait: I was going to tell the rest to you.
The queen learned how he was received abroad;

And, prompted by Christina (who, you know,
Is fond of patronizing all the arts),
Most graciously again has summoned him.

EVERARD.

This Ministry has seen its fairest days.

GENTLEMAN.

They say Alancia would not return
Till he had gained the pardon of the rest.
'Tis thought the leaders of the late revolt
Will be put into office by the queen;
They're men of broad and liberal statesmanship:
'Twill be a glorious time indeed for Spain.
[*He takes out his watch.*
How now? 'tis after twelve o'clock, — good day.
[*He hurries off.*

EVERARD (*he sits silent some minutes, then springs up, and walks up and down the room*).

She knows it: she had seen him yesterday.
Yes: that is why she came in pale and trembling;
I thought 'twas but a silly, girlish passion.

Zounds! how she must have longed to rid herself
Of my fair presence! I hung round her like
A buzzing moth, officious, while she flickered.

The furies take this fellow! he is back,
And handsomer than ever, I will swear,

But ah! he has done more than *look* well, too,
Yes, that's the worst of it, the worst of it;
'Tis what she would admire, — ah, Eleanor!

[*He stands lost in thought.*

Why should she marry me instead of him?

"Stuff," would Sir Henry say, — and so would I
A day ago. *Is* he the man they say?
Perhaps 'tis only honorable seeming,
Which the next idle wind of politics
Will puff away, and show a poor, thin schemer.
I'll dangle no more for her chary hand:
Sir Henry — he may rave it out as best
It suits him, —
Stop: I thought you cared for her.
Would you not serve a lady, Everard?
A lady whom you do profess to — love?

[*He walks up and down vehemently.*

Will you stand backward, like a sullen churl,
And let her brave the old man's disappointment?
Nor lift your finger, when you might, — you might
Make things run smooth between these sorry lovers?

[*He stops walking.*

I have some influence with Sir Henry; yes,
My words are law and gospel truth to him.

She never loved me; but she taught me still,
She taught me to despise my worldly aims.
And yet I am not bad as goes the world:

My heart was true whene'er it beat for her;
I thought that I could make her care for me.

[*He walks up and down again.*

No, no: I'll give her up, I'll give her up,
She never dreamed how much I reverenced her.
Can I make happiness? how would it seem?
An occupation rather new for me.
They say it is a very pleasant feeling.

[*He ponders.*

The duke shall have her, if my tongue avails;
And I — shall dry up in diplomacy,
And so live on, in gloomy bach'lorhood.
No woman did I ever love before:
I had no tongue to prove it, like this man;
I had no grace to show it, as this Spaniard.
No, no: he's worthy; I'll have done with this.

[*He dashes away a tear, and goes out.*

SCENE VIII.

In the parlor of the DUKE OF ALANCIA. EVERARD *is seated there alone, awaiting the entrance of the duke. The duke enters, bowing, but with great hauteur.*

THE DUKE (EVERARD *rising*).

Señor, be seated; and to what am I
Indebted for the honor of this visit?

EVERARD.

I came to speak to you, sir, of a matter
To which, I think, you're not indifferent.

THE DUKE.

What has your excellency, then, to say?

EVERARD.

I left Sir Henry Iverton to-day,
After some lengthy conversation with him.

THE DUKE.

Why am I privileged to know, señor?

EVERARD.

There is no use, sir, to disguise the truth
That brings me on my errand here to-day.
I know the sentiments Sir Henry's niece
Has entertained for you, and yours for her.

I have renounced, this morning, all my right
Unto the hand of my affianced bride!

THE DUKE (*springing up*).

Señor, I understand not what you mean.

EVERARD.

My words are plain, sir; take them as they are:
I argued with Sir Henry at some length.
He is inflexible, you are aware,
Concerning notions preconceived at first.
I am his friend: he holds me in his favor,
And gives me, as you know, the preference.
But I succeeded in convincing him
Of my unalterable determination.

I had the honor, also, to declare
(If you will pardon the opinion given),
That I believed you worthy of that lady,
Whom I do hold in high esteem as you.

ALANCIA.

Señor, señor! I cannot now accept
Your overwhelming magnanimity:
The lady gave her own consent to you.

EVERARD.

'Tis true, I never forced my suit upon her,
Nor took advantage of her uncle's favor;

But I am well aware she entertains
For you a feeling she has not for me.
It needed but a short experience

[*His voice wavers a little.*

To prove to me what I have often feared,
But never had acknowledged heretofore.

THE DUKE.

I stand abashed before you, caballero.
I have not had the honor, until now,
To know you ; else I had not so mistaken :
I have been interfering with your rights ;
I've met the lady since you were betrothed.
'Twas not her fault — 'twas not her fault, señor ;
I threw myself upon her unawares.
I only meant to own myself her slave,
And look my last upon her loveliness ;
But, when I saw her, passion led me on
To urge her to retract her vows to you,
And fly with me.

EVERARD.

Sir, that was natural.

THE DUKE.

It is a pleasure to revere, señor,
The man who did possess Elena's hand.
As for myself, I stand most low before

Your high and noble generosity:
It was my fortune, never my deserts,
If I had once the lady's preference.
I shall not now presume to press my suit;
I will not stand in rivalry beside
So true and honorable a gentleman.

I pray you to present yourself again.
[*His voice softens.*
Make known to her your generous resolve:
I stand apart. If you do win her yet,
I shall be proud, señor, of her approval;
And I shall ever, ever, entertain
A high regard for your exalted friendship.

EVERARD.

You overrate my deeds, I must assure you:
I do but yield unto necessity.

THE DUKE.

Your excellency's modesty forbids
That you should see your conduct in the light
I ever shall most gratefully regard it.
Should I possess the prize you do renounce,
'Twill be because high Heaven has decreed
Such benediction on my favored head;
And not because I have superior right,
Or equal, even, with your excellency.

EVERARD (*rising up to go, and holding out his hand hastily*).

I wish you, señor duke, all happiness.

THE DUKE (*grasping it*).

Señor, will you not leave *her* to decide?

[EVERARD *takes his hat, bows, and hurries out.* THE DUKE *looks after him confusedly, stands transfixed awhile, then smiles, runs about, hums a tune, and sits down.*

Certes, I am a miserable knave,
To triumph o'er this noble gentleman:
Yet 'tis not I that take her from his arms;
If she would rather fly unto this breast,
'Tis no offence of mine. Should she not choose?
He is a gallant man as e'er uprose
Amid the breezes of the north, and felt
The sea blow fresh upon his honest cheek.
Maybe the winds have made his manners cold,
And not for thee, my gentle, sweet Elena.
Thou wast afraid, who dost ingenuous speak
The kindling thoughts that fire thy earnest breast.
He chilled thee: but I see, beneath his look,
A heart too strong for little, common joys
Of other men. I love him for thy sake,
Because he laid himself beneath thy feet,
And silent rose again and went his way,
And bade me call thy every smile my own.

SCENE IX.

At Sir Henry Iverton's *hotel.* Everard *and* Eleanor.

EVERARD.

Eleanor, I am come to you to-night
On errand strange from gentleman to lady, —
A gentleman who in sincerity,
Hath laid most loyally his heart and hand
Before the kind disposal of his mistress:
I wish (if you will pardon my abruptness
In entering on the theme that brings me here)
No more to hold the hand that honored me,
But wholly to release you from the tie,
The obligation binding you of late.

ELEANOR (*turning pale*).

I know not what to say: explain your words.

EVERARD.

I never wished to force my suit upon you;
I had but little grace to speed my cause,
And less, far less, of real desert, except
An admiration most sincere for her
Whose hand I rashly dared to call my own;
And, if Sir Henry has ungently urged
And forced you on unto the step you took,
I was most ignorant of it indeed.

I feared you had but little love for me:
But then what lover ever ceased to hope
To rouse a feeling in his lady's breast.

[*She tries to speak, but her voice fails her.*

But stay, — of this no more: I wish to speak
To you of Manuel de Alancia.

[*She starts, and blushes deeply.*

Pardon: I have no suavity, you know;
I speak the thoughts that move me uppermost.

For many weeks I knew the duke to be
Your passionate admirer, Eleanor;
But now I know far more than this, — I know
He is a true and gallant gentleman.

[*She looks up astonished.*

Your uncle did not know his worth, nor I;
But now he cannot stop his ears to all
The honorable things they say of him:
His noble bearing towards the government,
And bravest maintenance of liberty.

[*She bows her head down.*

I wish to have Sir Henry meet the duke.

ELEANOR (*looks up blushing*).

You know Alancia? you — like him too?

EVERARD.

Yes: and may I present him to your uncle?

ELEANOR.

He is not changed, I think, since he came back.

[*She suddenly blushes deeply.*

EVERARD.

Do not be troubled: he has told me all;

'Twill do no harm to show him to your uncle.

[*She looks up suspiciously.*

EVERARD (*gravely*).

You think that I am *jesting*, Eleanor.

ELEANOR.

No, no.

[*Putting her hand to her head.*

But all is strange, as if I dreamed.

EVERARD.

Rough mediator am I, Eleanor;
But I do mean to serve you in my way.

ELEANOR.

My uncle knows him: they have met before.

EVERARD.

But I am proud to say he'll value one
I call my friend; he honors me so much.

[*She looks up amazed.*

'Tis true, — as such I claim Alancia.

ELEANOR (*a new meaning comes over her face; she springs up; grasps his hand*).

I shall not prove ungrateful for your kindness,
Nor soon forget your dealing with my heart,
For now I look on you with clearer eyes.

I did you great injustice, greatest wrong:
Not that I could not give my love to you.
You need not that: a little thing is that

[*He trembles slightly.*

For one who doth possess within himself
Such nobleness as now I see is yours;
But 'tis a sad mistake that I have made,
Beginning now so late to know your heart.

EVERARD (*his voice wavering.*)

No, no: I fear you saw me but too well;
I have not lived for goodness, Eleanor.
If I have loved the beautiful and good,
It is because I saw it all in you;
And learned, in company so pure and high,
There's something more than honors and ambition.
Your face it was that made me oft forget
The vexing *rôle* of the diplomatist.

[*The tears run down her cheeks.*

EVERARD (*turning his head aside quickly*).

May I present the duke this evening, then?

ELEANOR (*looking at him earnestly*).

I was but thinking how I wished that you
Might find some one to share your noble heart:
I pray you will not suffer long the thought
Of me to mar your peace and happiness.
I did not rightly e'en deserve your heart,
Seeing I so mistook its impulses.
Oh! make me happy, and distrust no more
My sex, but seek them in an honest faith;
And you shall find a true reward for love.
Reveal your gentler self in earnestness:
You cannot fail to win a woman's heart,
A constant heart, to beat for you till death.

EVERARD.

I have frequented many different scenes,
But I have met far other hearts than these:
They pleased me not before, — how shall they now,
Since I have seen and known you, Eleanor?

[*He rises hurriedly to go. She goes after him, and takes his hand.*

ELEANOR.

Grant me the privilege to be your friend;
Forgive me that I have disturbed your life;
Forget the most ungracious part I played;
And think that I shall name you in my prayers,
With supplications for your happiness,
And grateful memory of your noble friendship.

[*He lifts her hand to his lips, kisses it, and silently walks out of the room. Exit* ELEANOR.

SCENE X.

SIR HENRY IVERTON *in his apartment. Enter* EVERARD, *and behind him the* DUKE OF ALANCIA.

EVERARD.

Allow me, sir, to introduce to you
A gentleman whom you have met before,
Who asks the honor of this presentation.

Sir Henry Iverton, your excellency, —
The noble señor, Duke of Alancia.

SIR HENRY.

Be seated, sir: I hope you find yourself
In health since your return to Spanish soil.

ALANCIA.

I thank your excellency, I am well.

SIR HENRY.

You come from Italy, I think they say?
You must have passed a pleasant winter there.

ALANCIA.

Perhaps your excellency will remember
We had the pleasure, several times, to meet
Just at the close of winter here. The spring
I passed in Italy.

SIR HENRY (*coughing*).

True, true: your pardon.
How looked the vines? As well as here in Spain?
Our season opened most auspiciously.

ALANCIA.

Yes, all is blooming here; but yet I think
That Naples is fit match for Andalusia.
[*A long pause.*

SIR HENRY.

You go ere long to Madrid, I suppose?

ALANCIA.

I do not yet decide.

EVERARD.

Sevilla, duke,
Was once your home, I think I heard them say?

ALANCIA.

Yes: many years of youth I idled here.

EVERARD.

You do not find it changed, I fancy, either?

ALANCIA (*smiling*).

No: one's not often pained that way in Spain.

EVERARD.

So much the better for the traveller.

SIR HENRY.

Yes, if his bones will hold out on the way.

[*He goes impatiently to the window, throws back the curtain, looks out.* EVERARD *looks significantly at the* DUKE. SIR HENRY *turns round.*

ALANCIA (*his face flushing*).

Sir Henry, may I ask a favor of you, —
A few words private with your excellency?

SIR HENRY (*stiffly*).

Of course, sir, if you wish; step on this way.

[*They go into an adjoining room.* SIR HENRY *sits down.* ALANCIA *remains standing.*

Sit down, sir, if you please. How can I serve you?

ALANCIA (*seating himself*).

You have more power than will, I fear, señor.

[*He hesitates.*

Your excellency knows that I have loved
The Señorita Eleanor, your niece,
Since first I had the joy to see her face,
And feel her perfect loveliness of soul.

SIR HENRY.

I hoped, sir, that your absence had dispelled
In both a fancy which you must, ere this,
Have seen it was not wise for you to cherish.

[*His brow clouds.*

ALANCIA.

Your excellency —

SIR HENRY (*interrupting*).

You're aware, sir duke,
Not long ago Miss Manton was betrothed
To one whose hand she freely did accept.
To-day, that gentleman comes here to me,
With some nice point of honor, and declines
To keep her hand.
My lord, it is a strange,
A hard position, that I hold. I know
He is unchanged in feeling towards my niece.
What am I then to think of this, sir duke?
Looks it quite right another gentleman
Should step between, and break up, all at once,
Relations heretofore so fair and peaceful?

ALANCIA (*flushing hot*).

Señor, pray tell me, were both sides so fair?

SIR HENRY (*with irritated voice*).

I know what you would say about my niece.
The Señor Everard gives up her hand,
Because he thinks another's title better.
What right has he to give her up, señor?
If he is so magnanimous, my lord,
As to make way for — other gentlemen,
And yield his rights, *I* will not suffer it,
Nor let them reap from such a sacrifice.

ALANCIA.

So, please your excellency, I disdain
To found a single hope upon the words
Or generous actions of that gentleman,
Howe'er so much he puts me in his debt.
Señor, I hang not craven on his kindness:
I throw myself upon *her* verdict. Yes:
Where, in the name of Heaven, should be the place
To go for judgment but the heart itself, —
The lady's heart? What else should dare decide?
I know the world decrees a different sentence:
What business has the world with love? Good God!
I would its passion might set fire the world,
And burn up all its wretched heartlessness.

Your excellency, this brave gentleman
Possessed the right your favor did ensure;
He had no more, though high his merits were.
Love comes but at the bidding of the soul,
That says, "thou shalt," and none can turn its choice,
Nor set another form before the eyes.
  Señor, I have the first, divinest right,
Until this lady shall herself gainsay.

SIR HENRY.

You talk of love, — love is not all of life:
I have more years than you. You cannot feed
Upon the passion of a few months' growth,
Through all the future days in store for you;

For we must live and work, and eat and drink.

[ALANCIA *tries to speak.*

I ask not that a man should love my niece,
For that is easy; but that he protect her.
I know my friend. You, sir, I do not know.

ALANCIA (*springing up*).

You doubt my honor as a gentleman?

SIR HENRY.

That is your own construction, sir.

ALANCIA.

Señor,
I have a name no lady need to scorn:
Perhaps you mean that I am poor. 'Tis true
My father left me no inheritance;
But I believe that I can earn my bread.
I have abilities, however small,
By which I can command sufficient fortune.

SIR HENRY (*his face relaxing*).

I recollect, sir, now; I heard them speak
Of your most noble bearing towards the queen.

[ALANCIA *makes no answer.*

I am not slow to estimate you, sir,
On that occasion, as you well deserve.

ALANCIA (*after some silence*).

'Tis true I am of different tongue and nation;
I am a stranger to your family;
You care not if I be alive or dead.
'Tis natural; and I should not presume
To stand before you here, if there were not
Another view. The Lady Eleanor
[*His voice wavers*..
Looks on me with a different eye; at least,
I think she careth somewhat for my fate.
The fault is that we love, your excellency;
And that is my excuse for being here.
I cannot now think meanly of myself,
Since she has condescended to regard me.

SIR HENRY (*after musing awhile*).

Sir, I believe in you: I do respect
Your sentiments. As for my child, 'tis hard.
I blame you not, Duke of Alancia;
But I hold dear my little Eleanor.
I thought to see her look up to my friend,
And lean on him, when I am gone from her.
You love your race, sir; so do I love mine:
This mixture (pardon me) of foreign bloods
Creates dissension, bitterness, and sorrow,
So on, unto the ending of the chapter.
This is the common story of the world.
Can I believe that you and she will prove
A fair exception to all other lovers?

ALANCIA.

Ay, señor; for, although our blood be strange,
Our souls are not. We shall be closer knit
Than many, many lovers who arise
And look upon the dawn of life together.
   But, if we walk apart, we shall, indeed,
Be foreigners and pilgrims on the earth,
With no abiding place. Our home is love, —
'Tis wide, familiar, sweet, — our native home!
Nor she nor I are alien there, señor.

[SIR HENRY *sits silent.*

ALANCIA.

You have been young, Sir Henry, — you have loved.
Will not love make the different ways of life
Run smoother than the beaten path, with hate?

SIR HENRY (*he looks very grave, with his head down. Then he rises, and walks up and down the room. He talks, as to himself*).

Strange world; all things go wrong.
Perhaps 'twas I, — perhaps 'twas I went wrong,
These thirty years ago, or more maybe,
When I put those blue eyes from out my sight.
Because that I was poor, and they ambitious;
Because that I was proud, but she was not, —
She would have married me. Ah, well, well, well!

[*Musing aloud.*

And love should have its way, above all things.

ALANCIA (*starting up*).

Believe me, you shall not repent, señor.

SIR HENRY (*looking at him fixedly*).

Where is the little girl? I'll send for her:
I'll hear what she may have to answer you.

[*He rings the bell nervously, and summons her. Alancia starts up flushed, and paces back and forth. Presently she enters. She starts back, blushes, trembles. Alancia stands, and bows gravely.*

SIR HENRY.

Come here, my child: I wish to speak to you.

[*She goes to his table, and stands by him;* ALANCIA *standing apart.* SIR HENRY *lays his hand on her shoulder.*

The Duke of Alancia has offered you
His heart and hand, and what have you to say?
Answer me, do you love this gentleman?

ELEANOR.

Yes, sir: I loved him the first time we met.

[*She blushes.* ALANCIA *springs forward.*

SIR HENRY.

Stay, sir.
And are you willing, Eleanor,
To leave your home, your country, all for him?

ELEANOR.

Yes, sir.

SIR HENRY.

And you will gladly part from them,
Your friends who love you, Eleanor, — your uncle?

ELEANOR (*the tears falling*).

I am not glad unless I still may be
Your daughter, sir.

SIR HENRY.

The way is long between;
The land is strange and new to you, my child.

ELEANOR.

But I am not afraid, sir, where he is.

[ALANCIA *springs forward, kisses her hand, and goes back to the place where he stood.*

Dear uncle, I am not ungrateful, — no.

There are some things we cannot rule ourselves.
I did not mean to love a Spaniard, sir.

[*Smiling through tears.*

I meant to stay with you; but all this came,
Before I knew: yet, sir, he did no wrong;
I bade him hope through all the darkest hours.

[*Looking earnestly at* SIR HENRY.

Dear uncle, I can never cease to love you.

SIR HENRY (*dashing away a tear.*)

Take her, Alancia. Be tender of her;
For I may go away, and leave her here,

Amidst a land of foreign sights and sounds.
She thinks not of it now; she is in love;
She dreams of none but you; yet, by and by,
When we are far away, she'll talk of home.

Promise to be a true and watchful husband.

ALANCIA (*he springs forward, kisses the hand of* SIR HENRY, *and then draws* ELEANOR *to his side.*)

Señor, as I do hope for rest hereafter,
I swear to guard her faithfully till death.

SIR HENRY (*goes to the window to hide his emotion. He suddenly turns round*).

Where's Everard?

ALANCIA (*pointing to the parlor*).

Go bring him in, Elena.

[*She goes and draws him in gently by the arm.*

SIR HENRY (*goes up to him, and shakes his hand*).

Ah! my good fellow, we are plotting here
Against you all this time. But there's a place
For Everard in my house, and shall be ever.

ELEANOR.

He has a larger place in all our hearts.

[*Turning to* ALANCIA.

Thank him, Alancia, our noble friend,

ALANCIA.

Love him, Elena, as my benefactor.

ELEANOR (*going up to* EVERARD, *and taking his hand*).

You'll not forget us, now we've learned to prize you.

[*He raises her hand to his lips, and hurries out of the room.* ALANCIA *follows him.*

ELEANOR (*throwing herself upon* SIR HENRY'S *neck*).

Dear uncle, say that I am still your daughter,
Whatever dreary oceans roll between.

SIR HENRY (*kissing her*).

God bless and keep you ever safe, my child!

[ALANCIA *returns.*

ELEANOR (*putting her hand in his*).

Where is he?

ALANCIA.

He is gone, ah! my Elena.
We'll pray that some new joy may fall on him,
To light up all his days and hours like this,
With which our lives are glorified to-night.

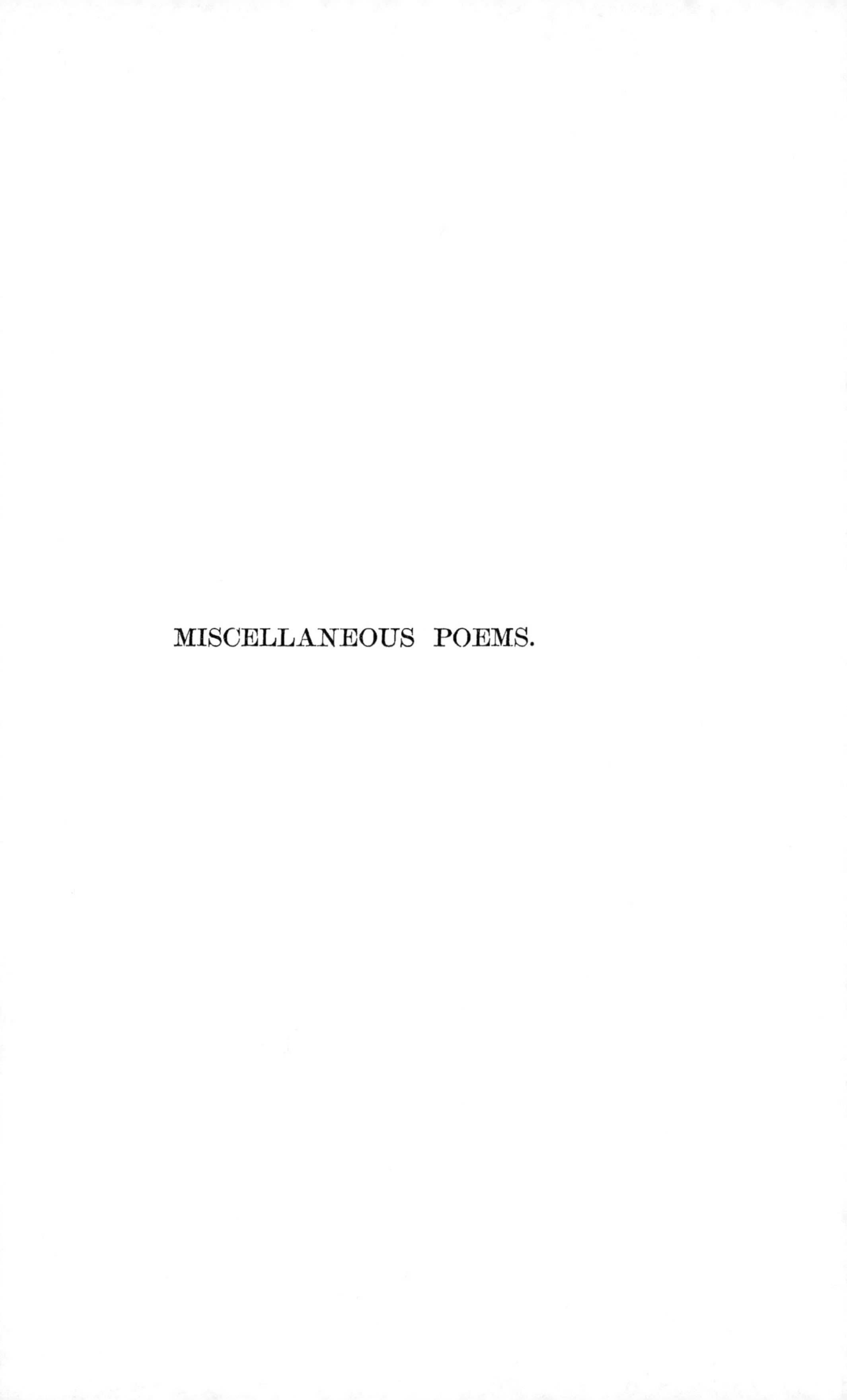

MISCELLANEOUS POEMS.

MISCELLANEOUS POEMS.

SPRING.

O SPRING! thou art a child of hopes and fears.
  What is thy nameless tenderness and grace?
  My heart is tremulous before thy face,
And but a look from thee will move my soul to tears.

Why should a breath of sadness on thee light,
  And such unuttered longings in thee wake?
  Hast thou not all, and more than all, to make
Thee richly blest — so loved and beautiful and bright?

The smiling flowers are sitting at thy feet,
  The birds are singing round thy head at dawn,
  The laggard sun now hastes to thee at morn,
And lingers fondly by thy side at evening sweet.

Art thou the type of higher blessedness?
  Because thou art like us of mortal mould,
  Must thou be ever yearning to behold
Perfection 'mid the fulness of thine earthly bliss?

THE MISTRESS OF THE "GOLDEN BEE."

THE sun was shining all the quiet day,
Upon the little inn, as there it lay,
And smiled the hours away.

I came in weariness to her retreat;
The dust of Lyons lingered on my feet,
And in my heart the heat.

She rose, and bent to me her gracious head.
"She had a charming room for me," she said.
And so the way she led.

I followed on, and ah! her words were true:
How peeped the curtained bed so white to view,
And fresh the air came through!

It opened on a court and parapet;
And there at eve my wicker chair I'd set,
And puff my cigarette.

She went away, — I heard her lightly spring
Along the tilèd floor, — and down I fling
    My sack, my every thing.

But, hark! she comes. "Monsieur must never wait
To sup with all the stranger guests at eight;
    Her tea was not so late.

And would I honor her?" I bowed my head.
"Too happy were I as her guest," I said,
    With soft, delicious dread.

"I'd know her room: 'twas by the shrubbery;
The yellow jessamine was climbing high,
    The parrot whistled nigh."

Away from out my longing sight she flashed,
And sang as merry as the fountain plashed,
    And on the myrtle dashed.

I turned me to the glass, and saw my face.
They said of old I had a kindly grace;
    But care had stolen its place.

My little fortune, gathered toilsomely,
Had dulled the gallantry of youth in me:
    Could I not gayer be?

I dressed me better than for many a day,
I shook my weariness and fear away,
And thought of what to say.

I found the open, vine-besprinkled door;
Her little boots were standing on the floor:
I looked them o'er and o'er.

She startêd from her alcove, gazed on me:
"Pardon, — the dew was wet, — how vexed was she
To have a stranger see!"

I watched them fly, — her pretty, stockinged feet;
She caught her crimson tapered slippers neat,
And gave me welcome sweet.

She sat at table with a pensive grace,
And asked of Paris: "'Twas a wicked place,"
"So gay," — and steeled her face.

A little tear she dropped that glimmered bright:
"She had no eye for any worldly sight;"
"Her heart was buried quite."

"She lost her Raymond but a year ago."
She was a widow, then! I longed to know
How bitter was her woe.

I prayed that I might be her loyal friend,
From all intruders on her walks defend,
And tears for Raymond lend.

She showered the sparkling diamonds from her eyes,
And looked at me in innocent surprise:
"Would I so sacrifice?"

She gave a flower she wore behind her brooch,
And called me "Cavalier" (me, so gauche!),
"Sans peur et sans reproche."

That night a fire was burning in my brain;
I turned upon my bed, and turned again:
I was in love, 'twas plain.

Ere long I told her all (I think she knew):
She helped me with a word or look, 'tis true.
Now all is clear to you —

How I am master of the "Golden Bee;"
For she is mistress of my heart, you see,
And both agree.

The rest you know, — how sweet the days go by,
Within the peaceful, airy hostelry,
Where she doth laugh and sigh,

And lure the traveller back with playful wile,
Or make him carry far away her smile
(She loves me all the while).

Our little "Golden Bee" is very fair:
Toil on, old aching world, I do not care.
Will you come there?

CLOVIS AND CLOTILDA,

KING AND QUEEN OF THE FRANKS.

"O QUEEN! my soul is weary of this life:
Where is the strength and glory of my days?
They fade away as doth an olden garment."
"Most noble king, it is because thy heart
Hath no secure and sweet abiding-place.
If thou wilt take the easy yoke of Christ,
Thou shalt go forward in thy kingdom singing."
"Talk not of this: I hate thy new religion.
See how it triumphed o'er the Roman state,
And now that haughty spirit, — how it lies
In dust and ashes at the spoiler's feet!
Could not thy glorified and risen Christ
Have saved his fairest jewel from the dust?
Is he so great? and yet the hordes of men
Have torn it from his crown and trampled it!"
"My lord, his kingdom is not of this world:
He loves the contrite spirit more than thrones.
He counts his followers every one by name,
And doth remember all his own in heaven."

"Clotilda, by the gods, thou wilt be there!
Where dost thou get thy gracious gentleness?
Thy piety is sweeter unto me
Than fairest groves of myrtle and of palm,
Than cooling water in the raging fight,
Than sound of music when the chase is done,
Than voices of thy children at the dawn.
What is it that doth honey so thy thoughts,
And sit in sovereign peace upon thy face?"
"Clovis, 'tis Jesus, — he of Nazareth."
"Clotilda, I will never hear his name;
I will fall down some day and worship thee,
But not this crucified and dying Christ,
Whose servants bite each other and devour,
And call it doing honor to his name."
"My lord, he says that men shall do these things
Because they know him not, nor him that sent him."
"Where is the child for whom thou once didst pray
Before me, O Clotilda! on thy knees
Beseeching that his forehead might be wet
With thy baptismal water? Where is he, —
That noble child, the offspring of my strength,
First-born of thine, — thy soul of tender fire,
Thy heart of innocence, thy brow of truth:
An eye that would have dared the sulky Roman,
And turned him from his silken hiding-place.
Where is the child? Cut down like April flower!
Was that the virtue of thy sacred water?
"My lord" (forgive my tears, — I am a woman),

"He is among the lambs of Paradise.
The grievous wolves are all about our flocks:
He is so safe, I would not call him back.
Make ready, gracious king, to meet him there."
"Ah, thou transcendent queen! where dwellest thou?
I plant my foot upon substantial earth;
I love the things I see, the sounds I hear;
If I possess them, then my soul is glad;
If I do lose them, then my heart is sore.
But thou art feeding on some hidden food;
The blossom of thy life is torn away;
Thou smil'st amid thy tears, and say'st 'tis well.
The roughening wars are beating at our doors:
Thine eye is patient with unending courage.
The sway of thy Redeemer waxes faint"—
"My lord, it shall not fail, though lands and thrones
Shall wither up in blackness as a scroll."
"Thou walkest surely in another world!
And yet not with the shadows of the dead;
For they are clinging round this mortal sphere,—
Unrestful spirits, longing for the flesh.
Thou art not there,—thine eye is calm and still:
But sometimes it doth look so far beyond,
I cannot follow, for my gaze is weak.
I turn again unto my mother earth
To rest my thoughts, and lo! I find thee there,
With all thy tender syllables of love:
Thy dainty handiwork, that orders well
The fair and sweet adorning of our lives,

And shows thee to thy people, wife and queen.
Where is thy strong retreat of living joy?"
"Thou wilt not hear the name of Jesus Christ."
"Ay, ay: since thou wilt speak it, I will hear."
"Canst thou walk lowly with him, my proud Clovis?
Canst thou, indeed, obey the crucified?"
"Ay: I will walk thy road, most noble queen,
No matter whither. If I find the light,
We two will then rejoice for evermore."

PIGEON COVE.

Lost! lost! lost!
O desolate sea,
I never can look upon thee!
I loved him when I was a child,
We frolicked together so wild
When we sat on the dripping rocks there,
And he hung the sea-moss in my hair.

He loved me, too,
So together we grew;
Till he asked me one day
When his ship was to sail far away,
If I "would not marry him when he came back"
('Twas his calling to follow the wide ocean's track).
"His heart would be warm in the stormiest night,
Could he dream of a welcoming light
One day in his home by the Cove,
To beckon him back to his love."

So I let him go:
My answer you know.
He bade me good-by,
With a light in his eye.
My lover! my lover! I saw his eyes light:
He never will look on my lamp shining bright.
The cold foam covered his beautiful head,
The cold foam lashed him until he was dead!

But stay, I will tell
How this sorrow befell:
The storm-wind came on, and the captain was sick;
My lover was mate: he bestirred himself quick,
And took the command;
He roused every hand.
He sprang to the mast, but his eye was not straight, —
The fever was on him of late, —
His knees trembled weak, —
Yet firmly they all heard him speak:
The order he gave,
Which the vessel did save.
Then he fell, — oh! he fell in the wave.

The ship dashed along,
And he was not strong;
Though well he could swim,
Yet the sea got the better of him.
Oh! had she been manned by the Pigeon-Cove men,
The waves had not swallowed him then.

The ocean repeateth his name,
For ever and ever the same.
I hear it at pale morning light,
It waketh me oft in the night.
The surf dashes up on the rock,
It sweeps on my soul with a shock.
That spring morning comes up again,
When they told me, — I knew it full plain, —
My father's lip trembled, and white grew his cheek,
And he laid his hand on me before he could speak.

'Twas the Spring when we thought to be wed;
Three month's have passed over my head.
The days grow sultry and hot,
I move in the very same spot;
The bathers go up and go down
Through the streets of the town,
And snuff the salt sea with delight;
But I hate the sight:
The waves of the sea
Are pointing their fingers at me.

But when winter cometh, oh! will it be sweet
To hear the wind driving and look at the sleet?
All day in the kitchen to sit
And braid on the matting, or knit;
And gaze on the ships in the bay,
Or dream how the icicles hang on the shrouds,
Where the white spray is driving in clouds,
And think of him drifting and drifting away?

No: the morning and evening are one,
The winter and fair summer's sun.
God! when will this living be done?

WORK.

Great Master! teach us how to hope in man:
  We lift our eyes upon his looks and ways,
  And disappointment chills us as we gaze,
Our dream of him so far the truth outran,
So far his deeds are ever falling short.
  And then we fold our graceful hands, and say,
  "The world is vulgar." Didst thou turn away,
O sacred spirit, delicately wrought!
Because the humble souls of Galilee
  Were tuned not to the music of thine own,
  And chimed not to the pulsing undertone
Which swelled thy loving bosom like a sea?
Shame thou our coldness, most Benignant Friend,
When we so daintily do condescend.

WORK.

Lord, send us forth among thy fields to work!
Shall we for words and names contending be,
Or lift our garments from the dust we see,
And all the noonday heat and burden shirk?
The fields are white for harvest: shall we stay
To find a bed of roses for the night,
And watch the far-off cloud that comes to sight,
Lest it should burst in showers upon our way?
Fling off, my soul, thy grasping self, and view
With generous ardor all thy brother's need;
Fling off thy thoughts of golden ease, and weed
A corner of thy Master's vineyard too.
The harvest of the world is great, indeed,
O Jesus! and the laborers are few.

THE WALK TOWARDS EMMAUS.

WALK with us, Jesus, when the day is spent:
  The robin's voice is full of tenderness,
  And all the air is silent with excess
Of sweet devotion, peace, and calm content.
Open our hearts that we may see aright
  The scripture of the world, — the burning page
  That shines upon our eyes from every age;
A fire to warn the sinner, but a light
  That gives the saint a glimpse beyond the veil.
Ask us, O Jesus! if we understand
The wondrous voices of the sea and land,
  As thou didst them who read the prophet's tale,
And knew not 'twas their blessed risen Lord, —
Read thou with us thy Father's hidden word.

"GO YE THEREFORE INTO THE HIGH-WAYS."

Church of Christ, awake to life, awake!
  Go to all the streets and lanes of sin;
Go, invite the homeless to partake, —
  Nay, compel them even to come in.

Have you now a blessed table spread,
  Where the Lord himself will come and eat?
Are your rightful members cold and dead?
  Let the halt and palsied have a seat.

They, in their unworthiness and fears,
  In their self-abasement low and deep,
Are like Mary seeing through her tears
  What a love the Shepherd bore the sheep.

It may be their presence at the feast
  Such a full refreshment will impart,
That your faith shall be the more increased,
  Springing deeper from the Master's heart.

Maybe their simplicity so meek
  Such a wakening will revive in you,
That your olden guests shall rise and speak,
  Saying, We have seen the Lord anew!

Sweetly thus may you in love abide,
  Till you rise together from the dead;
Poor and rich adoring side by side,
  One in Jesus Christ the Living Head.

THE BEAUTIFUL LADY.

WRITTEN FOR THE CHILDREN'S MISSION.

THERE is a gentle lady, very fair;
Her looks are saintly and her voice is rare;
    She walks through all the town,
    Nor fears to soil her gown.

They say this lovely lady's not afraid
Of any being that the Lord has made:
    She sees her Father's look
    Within the meanest nook.

And so she walks serene through every lane
Where hunger struggles fierce with sin and pain,
    And angry curses leap
    In passion wild and deep.

She does not even tremble at the sight:
She stands and gazes like a lily white,
    Till, awed to peace, they see
    Her spotless purity.

She stays beside the couch when all have fled,
And lays upon her breast the dying head,
    And sings away all fear
    With voice serene and clear.

She takes the little children in her arms,
And gives them bread to eat, and mildly calms
    Their throbbing hearts that beat,
    And wipes their bleeding feet.

Dear children, tell me, will you go with her, —
This lovely lady, each her messenger,
    And bid the orphans come,
    And have with her their home?

Her name, I think, is Charity below;
But, when her bright, immortal wings do grow,
    The angels there above
    In heaven will call her Love.

TO E. E. P.

WHEN I was walking in the hazy land,
  Midway betwixt my youth and womanhood,
That oped in vistas wide on every hand,
  With spots of glory faintly understood;

When all the air was faint with sweet perfumes,
  And golden halos hung 'mid earth and sky;
When I was steeped in tender lights and glooms,
  And heard the far-off voice of Poesy, —

'Twas thou, my sister, who didst speak and say,
  That I must tread the path which I have trod;
And thou didst never waver from the day
  Thou bad'st me be a singer to my God.

How have I answered to thy prophecies?
  We travel onward now in spheres apart:
New mounts of vision all around thee rise,
  Lit from thy children and thy husband's heart.

And I have wakened to a sweeter bliss
  Than all the ecstasy of poet-dreams;
But sometimes I would turn my eye from this,
  And see thy image in those morning gleams.

TO SHELLEY.

O RARE and evanescent spirit bright!
Even as the firefly skims along the night,
Men saw thee floating as a silver spark;
Then thou didst vanish sudden in the dark.

And yet the breath of evil fell on thee, —
The rude and venomous breath of calumny, —
Fell on a soul as pure and innocent
As God hath ever unto mortals lent.

When I behold thee, gentlest born of men,
The gracious sweetness dropping from thy pen,
I weep to think the world hath used thee so:
It cries to heaven, this spectacle below.

Could not thy gods, who kindly on thee smiled,
Have shielded thee, their strange and wayward child? —
Thee, with the dew of morning on thy hair,
The future mirrored on thy forehead fair?

They never lifted up a hand to break
The web of tyranny for thy sweet sake;
And yet the loveliness within thee grew
Transcendent in the fire men drove thee through.

Yea, verily, there is a God in heaven:
To know Him — unto thee it was not given;
He yearned to draw thee to his mighty breast,
And soothe thy weary, fluttering heart to rest.

Could He forget the soul which He had made?
So fair a soul would He have e'er betrayed?
Ah! He was kind; He stretched His arm to save,
When men were cold and cruel as the grave.

He laid thee in thy loving Ocean's arms,
Wrapt thee in joy amid the wild alarms,
Rocked thee to sleep, then gently bade thee wake,
And of another fairer life partake.

How softly drooped thy starry eyes away,
And closed for ever on the angry day!
How swift thy subtle spirit darted free,
And drank immortal love and liberty!

ELIZABETH BARRETT BROWNING.

Gentle woman, softly as the spheres
Move along the solemn, mystic years,
Thou didst tread alone thy path of tears,

Whispering yearnings from thy spirit deeps, —
Like a hidden mountain stream that creeps,
Darkly, secretly, before it leaps;

Sobbing lightly with its own unrest,
Groping blindly on the cold earth's breast,
Sinking downward, weary and oppressed.

Lowly bent the world its waiting ear,
For that undertone it loved to hear,
Listening with a strange and charmèd fear.

How at last the fountain leaped in light, —
Leaped with sudden joy, impassioned, bright,
When its sun of love arose to sight!

Proudly did the souls of men outreach,
Drinking in that lyric, burning speech,
When two poets melted each in each.

Then in wider music they did break, —
Music strong and grand enough to make
All the powers of wrong and falsehood shake.

Sing, immortal woman-poet, sing,
Where, with Dante, thou thy harp shalt bring,
On the sacred mountains of thy King!

Love, undying heart! Thou hadst not beat
If thy fragile pulses were not sweet
With a love thou couldst not all repeat.

Rest, elect and Christian lady, rest!
Where the saints and martyrs stand confessed,
Thou shalt be for evermore a guest.

Peace a halo on thy brow shall drop;
Peace, the perfect fulness of thy cup;
Peace, that ever bears thee higher up.

ARY SCHEFFER.

DEAR Artist, thou hast gone unto His breast —
The Great Consoler — whom thou picturedst here,
As all the heavy-laden round him pressed,
And dropped their griefs before his answering tear.

Sweet Raphael painted wondrously and fair
The lovely joy that filled the Virgin's eyes;
Murillo sent her floating on the air,
Glowing in dark-eyed, innocent surprise.

Perchance with firmer hand than thou they drew,
Born in the rapturous age of thronèd beauty;
Great ministers, unswerving, ever true,
Shaping her sovereign laws in love and duty.

Perchance their colors burned with deeper light,
Fresh from the olden southern sun, who whiles
The long day by the artist's side till night,
Retouching oft with mellow, lingering smiles.

So be it. Of another time thou art.
Framed is thy spirit in another mould;
Its high expression telleth every heart
That we have deeper eyes than they of old.

And thou hast answered to the earnest cry
Which from a new and longing age hath broke;
That looketh back with tender, reverent eye,
But findeth not enough for her was spoke.

For, on thy canvas page, humanity
Becomes divine, 'mid pain and fear and weeping;
Or 'mid the fulness of great joy, when high
And sacred converse with the unseen 'tis keeping.

Ah! here thy masters tarry far behind,
To catch the lights and shades of earthly day,
While thou art looking deeper in, to find
The hues which o'er the land of souls do play.

Go on; for now, at length, thou dipp'st thy brush
In the immortal bloom of Paradise;
Their hues shall wane before thy ripening flush,
Till thou above them all transcendent rise.

POESY.

O POESY! thou art not mine:
'Tis I, sweet sovereign, who am thine;
I never thought to seize on thee:
'Tis thou, 'tis thou who art possessing me!

I, tempted, flung thee from my side
To watch a bubble rainbow-dyed;
It charmed me with a power so sweet,
I waked not till it burst beneath my feet.

I flung me back upon thy breast,
Humiliated and opprest;
I cried to thee, "Go not away,"
And thou didst turn again and with me stay.

I walked subdued beneath thine eye,
In truth's divinest liberty;
Though oft I stumbled, still I went
In meekness on the road where I was sent.

Thou gav'st the earth a radiant dress,
And touched it with thy tenderness;
When thou wast singing, oft I thought
A snatch of hymns immortal thou hadst caught.

One day there came a spirit bright,
Who made my being warm and light;
His name was Love: I looked to see
If thou wouldst turn thy injured gaze from me.

He led me by the hand and smiled,
And pointed upward: pleased and mild,
Thou took'st my other hand, and so
Between you both the way to heaven I go.

THE SHADOW OVER THE LAND.

Poems written during the Rebellion.

THE SHADOW OVER THE LAND.

TO THE SISTERS OF THE SOUTH.

JAN. 1, 1861.

O SISTERS! where can be the wrong?
  No more, you say, shall we be one:
Yet we have tried to please you long,
  And all your bidding we have done.

We thought the only weight that lay
  Upon the pinions of your pride
You would outgrow and thrust away,
  If we should cheer you at your side.

Our share of work we asked to take,
  Presuming not to change your way,
But hoping, for your children's sake,
  The dawn of a more perfect day.

Perhaps we interfered too much,
But, ah! we meant it in good grace;
When, lo! you rose up at our touch,
And flung the gauntlet in our face.

O day of darkness, black as death,
When children turn in wrath and shame
Upon the home that gave them breath,
And trample on its sacred name!

Benignant Stars and Stripes, arise,
And call the wanderers from their track!
Look on them with indulgent eyes,
And say to them, "Come back, come back."

Forget, O noble flag, thy right,
Thy dignity and majesty!
Forget thy sovereign power and might,
All but the great Eternal Eye!

But if they will not put their trust
In thee, unless thou stoop'st so low,
That Freedom drabbles in the dust, —
For evermore, then, let them go!

Dread flag, let them in peace depart,
No drop of blood upon the sod!
Shall sister pierce her sister's heart?
Forbid — forbid it, mighty God!

Go, sisters, if it must be so;
  We wish you heartily God-speed:
If we no common country know,
  Let us not hate in word or deed.

You have a land like fair Provence,
  The goodliest of our fathers' share;
But over your inheritance
  Have you a care — have you a care!

Should servile Fury ever leap
  In havoc on your beauteous home,
We will not sit and see it sweep;
  Call us, O South! and we will come.

TO ARMS!

April, 1861.

TRAITORS and foes! We shall arm, we shall arm:
Brethren are ye? but it matters us not:
Men of the South! we are calm, we are calm:
Ye are like madmen, insulting and hot.

Long have we patiently borne with your hate;
Shame has been rising and flushing our brow:
Oh! we've entreated you, early and late;
God only knows what has come o'er us now.

We are not angry, — the fire is too deep;
We will not taunt, — that's for boys, and not men:
Yet we have sworn, and our word we will keep,
Never shall you trample on us again.

You have dishonored the Stripes and the Stars;
The pale North a moment did hold in her breath:
Now thousands of eyes, like the red planet Mars,
Do glare on you steady defiance and death.

You love not to work, — you are all gentlemen;
  Arms are your pastime, and "fight" is your word:
We love the plough and the loom and the pen;
  Nobler is peace to our hearts than the sword.

You have been plotting all over the land;
  You have been training to tear down the state:
We've not been playing with weapons in hand,
  But we'll tear down your flag at the capital's gate.

Lord of the nations, restrain us, — restrain!
  Terrible, mighty, our waking at last:
Tears, if they fall, shall come down like the rain,
  And flood the degenerate soil of the past.

But courage, ye men of the North and the West!
  A nation is springing again into birth;
In the radiant garments of Liberty dressed,
  A wonder of beauty all over the earth!

WHERE IS PEACE?

MAY 26, 1861.

THE earth is born anew to love and light;
The green is deepening on the wood and plain;
The birds are flitting gayly in our sight,
Or chirping in the gentle spring-tide rain:
But where, oh! where is peace?

The homes of men are growing chaste and fair;
The cherished maiden tends the budding vine;
The farmer drops the little seed with care,
And round his door the morning-glories twine:
But where, oh! where is peace?

The sick man, with a slow and measured tread,
Goes up and down the pleasant village street;
The neighbors think him risen from the dead;
He thinks that life and spring are very sweet:
But where, oh! where is peace?

The mountains sit majestical and free,
  And call the traveller to their sacred calms;
The sea is waiting most enchantingly
  To fold the idler in its glistening arms:
    But where, oh! where is peace?

The golden hours are dallying at our feet;
  They will not leave us till our joy is full;
And time is ours, — the time we called so fleet, —
  From early morning till the evening cool:
    But where, oh! where is peace?

Peace! Thou hast not departed from us now;
  Thou dost but take for us another mould:
I see thee sitting on the soldier's brow;
  His eye predicts thy reign of joys untold.

Shall we, like children, hug thy shadow here,
  And not a step beyond thee dare to take?
Shall we, like cowards, tremble in our fear,
  And never lift a sword for thy great sake?

Forbid it, all ye spirits of the dead!
  Forbid it, nations whom we came to save!
Forbid it, gentle spring! for thou dost shed
  Thy sweetest blossoms on the soldier's grave.

Benignant Peace! I see thee from afar,
  Beyond the tumult and the battle heat;
Amid the tears and bloody drops of war,
  I hear the music of thy coming feet:
      Ah! there, — ah! there is peace.

CAMPAIGN SONG,

(Before the Re-election of Abraham Lincoln),
Nov., 1864.

Fly upward, fly upward, high into the night,
Red rockets and blue, red rockets and blue!
Like the stars and the stripes, they are gleaming in light,
Then throw them anew; then throw them anew!

See the torches that wave on the gay city street, —
Red torches and blue, red torches and blue!
'Tis the flaming of Liberty's swift-coming feet:
Come out with her too; come out with her too!

See the orator stand at the top of the Square;
Hear, father and son; hear, father and son!
His sentences turn into fire on the air;
And the combat is won; the combat is won!

American soldiers, we ask you to fight,
But choose ye your chief; choose ye your chief;
The man who can show you the wrong from the right,
Though in words he is brief,—though in words he is brief.

Choose you, O maiden! the man you will wed;
  Not the man who will vote for the tongue that is smooth:
Not the man of a party, the man who is led;
  But the man for the truth, — the man for the truth.

Choose, nation, to win or surrender the day,
  To gain or to lose, — to gain or to lose.
Choose, voice of the people, for ever and aye,
  The freeman or slave, — choose, countrymen, choose!

THE PICTURE OF COLONEL SHAW, IN BOSTON.

NOVEMBER, 1864.

Buried with his negroes in the trench,
  There he lies, a score of them around him;
Nothing could his deathless ardor quench:
  What a monument at last has crowned him!

Sight to make a father's bosom throb,
  There he stands upon the canvas glowing;
Sight to make a noble mother sob,
  Tender eyes their glances on her throwing.

There he stands, so eloquent and mute,
  Modest, and yet looking in our faces
Undisturbed and calmly, — as doth suit
  One who did not ask the world's high places.

There he gazes, soldier-like and bold,
  Not a whit ashamed to die with them, —
Them, the men of color, bought and sold;
  Not a bit ashamed to lie with them.

Look upon him, nation of the free,
  Surely thou art cured of all thy meanness!
Look upon him, nation that's to be,
  Rising purified from thy uncleanness.

Sleep serenely with a people's sigh,
  Noble martyr to thy country given:
With thy little company on high,
  Thou shalt traverse all the plains of heaven.

OUR PRESIDENT.

April, 1865.

THE grass is growing green upon the hills,
The spring is loosening all the little rills,
A tender bloom is on the willow-tree:
  But where, oh! where is he?

Will he awake to-morrow with the day,
And turn his face the way the battle lay;
And thank the Lord that he has lived to see
  The triumph of the free?

O God, have pity on us! he is dead.
The foul assassin aimed at his dear head;
He never spoke a word to let us know
  How hard it was to go, —

To leave us at the crowning of our joys,
When we were praising gallant men and boys,
And shedding happy tears of sweet relief,
  And thanking him, our chief.

Weep, all ye dark-faced children of the sun!
He gave his blessing to you every one;
That blessing was a throe to all the earth, —
Emancipation's birth.

Weep, O misguided wretches, comfortless!
And wash away your gall of bitterness;
Have you not lost a noble friend and true
As ever stood by you?

Weep, mighty nation! who shall dare to say
That we are cowards for our tears to-day?
But let the drops be mingled with a fire
That burns all low desire, —

The fire that flashes light upon our path,
And purifies from vengeance and from wrath;
The fire of resolution, high and strong,
To grapple with the wrong.

Farewell, beloved father! sleep in dust;
But rise thou in the kingdom of the just, —
Beyond the traitor's breath, the battle scars, —
And shine among the stars!

LAY HIM TO REST.

April, 1865.

Lay him to rest, lay him deep in the ground;
Full long enough ye have borne him around,
With the tramp of the horse, and the weary drum-beat,
Before all the eyes and the glare of the street:
Lay him to rest.

They were eyes full of love, they were eyes that did weep,
And the chillness of death on the cities did creep;
But now, gentle friends, let him go to his rest, —
Let him go to his home in the heart of the West:
Lay him to rest.

Why did we take him from fair Illinois?
He was young in her woods, he was fresh as a boy;
Why did we set him high up in that place,
And bring all the furrows of care to his face?

Why do we send him back so to his land,
With a blood-mark upon him from traitorous hand?
Why do we show them the wound in his head,
And say not a word but "Behold! he is dead"?

We brought him from westward because he was just;
We made him our chieftain, we gave him our trust;
Serene in the midst of the tumult he stood,
And we learned that 'tis greatest of all to be good.

We've let him die for us, — yes, we've let him die,
With his armor all on, as the soldier boys lie,
Not a moment of warning — a message to tell;
And we say he sleeps well, and we say he sleeps well.

Be proud, Illinois, for to you it was given
To raise up the noblest of martyrs for heaven;
Be pure, Illinois, for now 'tis your part
To let this dear ashes repose on your heart;
Lay him to rest, lay him to rest,
On Illinois' breast.

BLIND TOM.

HE laid his childish hands upon the keys,
  And drew out snatches of melodious song;
He has no learning of the schools to please:
  His own sweet inspirations on him throng.

He sees in dreams behind his sightless eyes
  The glory of the children of the sun;
He sees them, like the god of day, arise,
  Rejoicing in the race which they shall run.

Ah, they have wakened from their bondage, Lord!
  Ere long, a wondrous harmony shall roll
Around the land, and touch a hidden chord
  Of sympathy within the white man's soul.

Will they not calm his pulse's feverish beat,
  And show him how religion's pleasant ways
Are better than the traffic of the street,
  And, best of all his gains, the Master's praise.

For he declared of old, in Galilee,
  That they who had the lowliness of love,
Even like the little child upon his knee,
  Were fittest for his Father's house above.

Poor little Tom! and so he played and played,
  And these the visions beautiful and bright
I thought he saw, beneath the darksome shade
  That closed around and shut him from the light.

THANKSGIVING.

Dec. 7, 1865.

God of nations! what a day,—
What a gift from thy dear hand!
Happy people went to pray,
Thanking thee all o'er the land.

Then they sought the festive board,—
Fathers with their little ones,
Mothers with the kisses stored
For their noble soldier sons.

Did we on that day forget
Him who led us through the sea,
Bearing toil and care and sweat,
That a nation might be free?

Spoke we not his martyr name
With a tender voice and calm?
Did it not subdue our game,
Like a reverent, household psalm?

Peace indeed has come at last!
She it is who sanctifies
All the anguish of the past;
All the light is from her eyes.

Sacred Peace, for ever stay,—
Still the fretful voice of care;
Drive our worldliness away,
Angel song upon the air!

Not thy treacherous counterpart
Some would have us take, forsooth,—
She, who, with a timorous heart,
Dares not strike a blow for truth.

But thy own resplendent face,
Gracious daughter of the sky!
Awing all the traitor race
With sublimest majesty.

Cambridge: Press of John Wilson and Son.

List of Publications

ISSUED AND FOR SALE BY

WILLIAM V. SPENCER,

203 Washington Street, Boston.

☞ *The usual Discount to the Trade.*☜

ANDERSON (I. H.) Patriotism at Home; or, The Young Invincibles. By the author of "Fred Freeland." With Four Illustrations, from original designs by CHAMPNEY. Printed on heavy paper, in handsome binding. 1 vol. 16mo. Price $1.50.

BERRY (MRS. M. E.) Celesta. A Girl's Book. 16mo. In press. $1.25.

——— Crooked and Straight. 16mo. In press. $1.25.

BRADLEE (MISS). Christus Victor. A Poem. Square 16mo. Flexible cloth. 50 cts.

——— Max Overman. 16mo. Paper. 50 cts.

——— Three Crowns. 16mo. Cloth. $1.25.

BULFINCH (REV. S. G., D. D.) Manual of the Evidences of Christianity. For Classes and Private Reading. 12mo. $1.25.

CALVERT (G. H.) Some of the Thoughts of JOSEPH JOUBERT. With a Biographical Notice. 16mo. Tinted paper. Cloth, bevelled. $1.50.

——— First Years in Europe. By the author of "Scenes and Thoughts in Europe," "The Gentleman," &c. 1 vol. 12mo. $1.75.

A finished and attractive narrative of a residence in Antwerp, Gottingen, Weimar, Edinburgh, and Paris, forty years ago; abounding in powerful criticisms of the religious and political sentiment of that time, exhibiting a close study of the literature and a familiar acquaintance with the literary men of that age.

CARPENTER (MISS MARY). Our Convicts. 2 vols. in 1. pp. 293 and 380. Octavo. $4.50.

CHANNING (MISS E. P.) The Adventures of a German Toy. A charming story for children, with three Illustrations. 75 cts.

COBBE (Frances Power). Religious Duty. 12mo. Cloth, bevelled sides. $1.75.

——— Studies New and Old, of Ethical and Social Subjects. Crown 8vo. Price $3.00.

Contents: Christian Ethics and the Ethics of Christ; Self-Development and Self-Abnegation; The Sacred Books of the Zoroastrians; The Philosophy of the Poor Laws; The Rights of Man and the Claims of Brutes; The Morals of Literature; The Hierarchy of Art; Decemnovenarianism; Hades.

FERNALD (Rev. W. M.) God in his Providence. 12mo. Cloth. $1.50.

——— A View at the Foundations; or, First Causes of Character. 12mo. Cloth. $1.00.

GREY (Hester). Kitty Barton. A simple Story for Children. With One Illustration. 32mo. 60 cts.

HOLLISTER (G. H.) Thomas à Becket. A Tragedy, and other Poems. 16mo. $1.75.

LINCOLNIANA. In one vol., small quarto. pp. viii. and 344. $6.00. (Only 250 copies printed.)

MARTINEAU (Jas.) Essays: Philosophical and Theological. Crown Octavo. Tinted paper. $2.50.

☞ Other volumes of the series in preparation.

MILL (John Stuart). Dissertations and Discussions. 3 vols. 12mo. Cloth. Per vol., $2.25.

——— The Examination of the Philosophy of Sir William Hamilton. 2 vols. 12mo. Cloth. Per vol., $2.25.

——— The Positive Philosophy of Auguste Comte. 1 vol. 12mo. Cloth. $1.25.

MUZZEY (Rev. A. B.) The Blade and the Ear. Thoughts for a Young Man. 16mo. Red edges, bevelled sides, $1.50; plain, $1.25.

NAVILLE (Ernest). The Heavenly Father: Lectures on Modern Atheism. By Ernest Naville, late Professor of Philosophy in the University of Geneva. Translated from the French, by Henry Dornton, M. A. Published in a handsome 16mo volume. $1.75.

"A thorough grappling with some of the most subtle and profound questions of the age. 'The Revival of Atheism,' &c. The author is thoroughly evangelical, and has treated his subjects with a masterly scholarship and ability. We hail all such books as the fulfilment of the Scripture promise, 'When the enemy shall come in like a flood, the spirit of the Lord shall lift up a standard against him.'"

REED (Wm. Howell). Hospital Life in the Army of the Potomac. 16mo. $1.25.

STAHR (Adolf). The Life and Works of Gotthold Ephraim Lessing. Translated from the German of Adolf Stahr, by E. P. Evans, Ph. D., Michigan University. 2 vols. Crown octavo. $5.00.

THURSTON (Mrs. Elizabeth A.) The Little Wrinkled Old Man. A Christmas Extravaganza, and other Trifles. Illustrated. 75 cts.

TOWLE (Geo. M.) Glimpses of History. 1 vol. 16mo. Bevelled boards. $1.50.

TOWNSEND (Miss Virginia F.) Darryll Gap; or, Whether it Paid. A Novel. 1 vol. 12mo. pp. 456. $1.75.

A book of great force and power, dealing with the follies, the errors, and the extravagance of this great sensational age. Depicting life among those who have suddenly acquired wealth, and displaying lessons of devotion and self-sacrifice, drawn from a new field, hitherto untrod by the novelist. The *Boston Transcript* says of it:—

"The story is thoroughly American in tone, scenery, incident, and characters; it is to American life what Miss Bremer's 'Home' is to life in Sweden. Like the Swedish tale, simple, natural in incident, its characters have each a powerful individuality which takes hold at once upon the interest and sympathies of the reader. The drama of the story is artistic, and though its materials are drawn from the simple, human, every-day life of our homes, the power of the book is felt to its close; the moral lessons it unobtrusively teaches, cannot fail to sink deep into the hearts of all who read it."

WARE (Rev. J. F. W.) Home Life: What it Is, and What it Needs. 16mo. Cloth. Red edges, bevelled sides. $1.25.

Recently Issued.

REASON IN RELIGION: By F. H. Hedge, D.D. 1 vol. Crown octavo. $2.00.

NEW WORKS JUST ISSUED.

LOVE IN SPAIN, AND OTHER POEMS. By Martha Perry Lowe. 1 vol. 16mo. $1.50.

SERMONS: By Rev. E. B. Hall, D.D., Pastor of the First Congregational Church, Providence, R.I., from 1832 to 1867. With a brief Memoir. 1 vol. 16mo. $1.25.

FIRST HISTORICAL TRANSFORMATIONS OF CHRISTIANITY. From the French of Athanase Coquerel the Younger. By E. P. Evans, Ph.D., Michigan University. 1 vol. 16mo. $1.50.

*** Copies sent by mail, free of postage, on receipt of price.

THE LIFE AND WORKS

OF

LESSING.

TRANSLATED FROM THE GERMAN OF ADOLPH STAHR, BY E. P. EVANS, PH. D., MICHIGAN UNIVERSITY.

Two volumes. Crown octavo. Price $5.00.

"A work of permanent value. . . . It is the best of many books which have been written and compiled for the purpose of portraying the character and career of one of the most illustrious scholars and thinkers that even Germany has produced. It combines judicious selection with ample information, criticism with narration, and presents with comparative brevity an outline of labors, the benefits of which the world is now enjoying in almost every department of learning and culture. . . . The translation is excellent."—*Nation, New York.*

"The position of Lessing in German literature renders him the subject of peculiar interest among those who have at heart a sound intellectual culture in this country. We are thankful to Professor Evans for presenting to our countrymen the biography of such a man in so handsome a form. . . . We can safely predict to our readers that the perusal of the volumes will give them a fresh sympathy with a man whose name has to a great extent been the subject of vague association rather than positive knowledge, and will throw new light on the fortunes of the great battle for freedom and truth in the last century."—*New York Tribune.*

"As a literary biography, it is one of the best specimens which has appeared in many years, and seems to have been a labor of love to both author and translator. We commend these handsome, valuable, and interesting volumes to all inquiring, progressive, and sympathetic minds, and all readers who would become familiar with the noblest type of literary life."—*N Y. Independent.*

"Stahr's biography of Lessing, which he has so admirably translated in these volumes, was the result of 'twenty years of earnest and enthusiastic study.' It is an elaborate account of Lessing's life, works and times, influence and contemporaries, and is a valuable contribution to the literary history of Germany."—*Boston Transcript.*

"A highly honorable contribution to American letters."—*N. Y. Tribune.*

For sale by all booksellers. Copies sent by mail free of postage, on receipt of retail price.

A liberal discount allowed to libraries, students, and clergymen.

WILLIAM V. SPENCER,

PUBLISHER,

203 Washington Street, corner of Bromfield.

www.ingramcontent.com/pod-product-compliance
Lightning Source LLC
LaVergne TN
LVHW050518100826
845148LV00002B/380

9781425520472